How To Investigate Your Friends And Enemies

BY LOUIS J. ROSE

Illustrations by Edward Kohorst

Published by: Albion Press
            582 Stratford Ave.
            St. Louis, Mo. 63130

ISBN: 0-9606846-2-X

Library of Congress Catalogue Card Number: 81-68851

Printed in the United States

First Printing: September 1981

First Revised Printing: April 1982

Second Revised Printing: January 1983

Third Revised Printing: January 1992

This edition dedicated to
Neil Edward Rose
(1967–1989)

CONTENTS

PREFACE

ARE YOU considering a business deal with someone who exudes sincerity but about whom you have misgivings?

Is some government agency or bureaucrat giving you a hard time for no apparent reason? Are others getting favored treatment when you're not?

Do you suspect that public officials in your community are enriching themselves at taxpayers' expense perhaps through land, zoning or banking deals? How can you check on them? Are public funds being wasted, with little or no accountability?

Have you or your organizaton been subject to secret surveillance, with dossiers being compiled on you by federal or police agencies?

This book can help you get the answers to such questions.

The title, "How to Investigate Your Friends and Enemies," was chosen because it is an apt one. In today's world, when we have business dealings with persons who may be mere acquaintances or even strangers, it often is important to learn as much about them as we can.

For example, are they the kind of person or company they seem to be? Are their assets what they would lead us to believe? What kind of record have they had in dealings with others? Are they to be trusted, or do we have to be on special alert in our relations with them?

If a government agency is involved, what kinds of records and data exist, and are we entitled to inspect such records? How much can we learn about people in general, without their knowledge?

This book is intended as a primer for persons who would like answers to these questions. If you would sometimes like to be your own private detective and do your own checking up, this book is for you.

Imagine yourself seated in a dark auditorium. Suddenly a door opens and a man enters through a dim light. You catch only a brief glimpse of him. "My name is John Gregory Simonds," he says. "I live in

Webster Groves, a St. Louis suburb."

He pauses, then walks out the same door he entered. Again there is only a brief glimpse in the dim light through the doorway. It suggests he may be in his 40s.

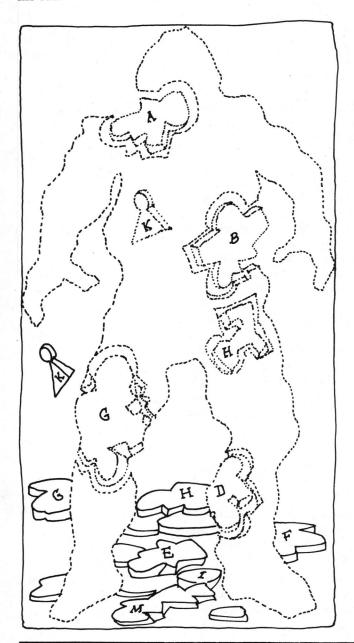

You know his name and where he is from, but nothing else about this stranger. What kind of a person is he? What does he do for a living? Is he married? What's his address, occupation, and what does he look like?

You should be able—with effort, imagination and a little luck—to find answers to all these questions and perhaps many more. It might surprise you to discover that you can learn not only his weight, the color of his eyes and his height, but also how affluent he is, what property he owns, his marital record and scores of other details about his public and private life.

All this without ever actually meeting or talking to John Gregory Simonds.

Your success may depend, in part, on the state or community he lives in. But the chances are better than good that you will be able to reconstruct the identity and life-style of such a person—or, better yet, a friend, casual acquaintance, enemy or a total stranger.

So too with public officials and governmental agencies.

Best of all, you can do it largely using only public records available to anybody.

In my 25 years as a newspaper reporter who has covered virtually every level of government and all types of news situations, I have gained some valuable insights. More than half my career has been spent as an investigative reporter. During that time, I have tried to pick up a lot of useful knowledge about the use of public and private records and investigative techniques.

Since the Watergate scandal of 1973-74 in which two reporters helped topple President Richard M. Nixon from office, a whole series of books have been written setting forth the techniques used by experienced investigators in the media and law enforcement. Too often, however, these publications have been aimed to those with some experience in the investigative field. They often are of little value to the average citizen, who lacks the background needed to check things out for himself.

In contrast, I have tried here to provide a concrete, step-by-step easily understood approach to investigative projects.

The approach includes more than just a primer. It also emphasizes your need to use your most valuable investigative weapon—your own mind.

Given the enormous array of situations, conditions or persons that you might want to investigate it is not enough to give case histories of investigations that have been successful. No one can provide a step-by-step approach that will meet every reader's needs.

But there is one likely key to success—your own intellect. I have tried in this book to show you how to use your creativity and imagination to do your own investigative work.

With help you can do it if you put your mind to work. The going may at times be tedious and frustrating. But just as often it also can be very productive as well as fun.

Some investigators won't tell you how they work and even refuse to share their methods and techniques with their colleagues. They like to create an aura of mystery about how they uncover information that others have sought to conceal. But they can do little that you could not duplicate, given the know-how and the time and effort.

What I have tried to do here is to let you in on some of their most treasured "secrets." Many of their secrets come out of public records available to you by law and at little, if any cost.

Louis J. Rose

St. Louis Mo.

I. The Nature of the Beast

Even in Computerized Times, Your Quarry Leaves a Trail

INVESTIGATIVE reporters and private detectives have long been with us. The art of investigation may be as old as mankind itself. The first investigator likely was a primitive man or woman who followed a trail or observed nature for signs of what happened.

Closer to our time, the American Indian and the frontier man advanced the art. They looked about them and found clues in broken branches, bent twigs, the charred remains of campfires and footprints of man and animals in the soil. We no longer live in a wilderness where such physical clues are so easily seen or relevant.

But our society now leaves more trails and more clues of a different type than any society before us. The art of tracking is far more advanced and sophisticated today than it was decades ago. We have become the truly programmed and computerized society .. a society littered with countless records. The records are not prints in the soil, but they are there, nevertheless.

Such records come to us roughly from three sources.

The first, and perhaps most enlightening, is a record, or document, source. As used here, the term record also applies to photographs, tape recordings, video recordings, or a combination of all these. Such records are everywhere about us. Consider just a few that we may encounter daily — bills, receipts, checks, letters, memos and reports. The list of such records can be endless.

Many of these records are available for us to inspect and evaluate. Others may not be easily accessible, but we can often get access to them if we have the determination and imagination.

The second source of information is people — anyone who provides information to you. It could be a neighbor, a fellow employee, a fireman, a drugstore clerk or a building inspector.

The third is the physical source. You observe something and from that you deduce what has happened — the broken branches and bent twigs that we cited earlier, for example.

If you enter a house and see an automobile protruding through a wall of the living room, you would say the automobile had smashed into the house. Similarly, if you saw two cars crumpled together on the street, you could assume there had been a collision.

First, let us dwell on record, or document, sources. These are perhaps the most prevalent sources of information that we have. The number and type of such written or printed records is increasing at a dizzying speed in our computerized society.

No one person, regardless of how expert he or she may be, can be familiar with all the types of records that are being generated. Hundreds of thousands of records and documents are produced daily in such fields as government, engineering, accounting,

"No one person, regardless of how expert, can be familiar with all types of records that are generated."

banking, insurance and an array of other enterprises. The volume is almost beyond comprehension.

The output of a single governmental unit — your city or county government, for example — might take a small-size book to catalog. Just a partial county list, for instance, might include:

—Property and land transfer deeds, mortgages, options

—Assessments and tax records, including liens and delinquencies

—Contracts, bid documents, advertisements for bids

—Minutes of county council meetings

—Election and campaign finance records

—Planning and zoning applications, permits and hearings

—Payrolls, budgets, expense vouchers, receipts, telephone bills

—Building and health inspection reports

—Cancelled checks or microfilm copies of every check issued in a given period

—Bond issue funds and payments

—Departmental revenue collections

—Franchise records, licenses and permits

—County bank depositories and investments

—Governmental committee reports, ordinances and audits

—Marriages, divorces, births and deaths

—Lawsuits, both civil and criminal, and police records

A full listing, even for a medium-sized county, might be far more extensive. Bureaucracies inevitably spawn paper work, often in triplicate. But the bureaucrat may be your best friend when you want to investigate something.

Blessed are the bureaucrats and their duplicate or triplicate copies.

No one person could be able to identify by number or other special code the title of a document he or she may want to examine. Most of us are all too familiar with form 1040 But there are few such records or

"Blessed are the bureaucrats and their duplicate and triplicate copies."

forms that we are able to identify by the title, number or description.

So how is it possible to find out what records exist, whether they are available and, if so, how they might be obtained?

As an investigative reporter, I have often been asked what is the most valuable tool an investigator can use. Modern technology has given us a dazzling cupboard of wondrous inventions and devices to help in investigations. Infra-red scopes allow police to pick out or track a suspect in the dark. Law enforcement officials can monitor the location and movement of vehicles, thanks to a little gadget attached surreptitiously to a car that one wants to track.

Electronic listening and eavesdropping devices are so sophisticated they can pick up sounds through a wall or across open spaces at surprising distances.

Anyone experienced in law enforcement could probably catalogue a variety of equipment useful in surveillance and investigation. So too could many experts aligned with the underworld, as well as experts in the field of business and industrial espionage.

Law enforcement officials often can legally use these devices. But, frequently, even they must obtain permission of the courts. Criminal and industrial spies don't worry about such niceties.

For most of us laymen and private citizens, however, the costs and legal issues involved prohibit our using them. But we have one not-so-secret intelligence-gathering marvel that is far more versatile and valuable than any gadget or gimmick. That weapon is our own mind.

The human mind, despite its flaws, is a wondrous resource. It can outperform any gimmick in the pursuit of information vital to our needs.

II. The Investigative Compulsion

A Sleuth, Real or Fictional, Must Have a Relentless Mind

NO matter how great their talents, ball players and musicians who don't practice or perform regularly lose that extra edge of skill. A car left too long unused or idle in a garage may not start or perform up to par. So too with the mind.

Our best-known giants in the investigative field are the mystery writers, whose works sell in the millions and have been translated into scores of languages. They have given us a parade of appealing super-sleuths—Sherlock Holmes, Hercule Poirot, Miss Marple, Lord Peter Wimsey, Lew Archer and Nero Wolfe.

Each possesses a common trait: Their single-minded compulsion to solve a puzzling mystery. They are driven to unravel the unknown. Their minds and instincts are their chief weapons.

Few real-life investigatiors achieve such fame. But their efforts are no less appreciated or admired. Detectives, both police and private, through long and painstaking work, have repeatedly brought the guilty to justice and freed the innocent.

Investigative journalists through the years have exposed wrongdoing and corruption. They have uncovered governmental scandals, political payoffs, business ripoffs, fake charities, bribery of public officials, labor and union corruption, as well as illegal banking and land-sale schemes. They have brought to public consciousness a grim litany of intolerable conditions and abuses in mental institutions, jails and the drug and food industries.

They have bared our hidden public shame.

The American tradition of investigative journalism traces back to the muckraking era in the 1800s and the early part of this century.

Giants of that era included Ida M. Tarbell, who was perhaps the greatest of the muckrakers, and Lincoln Steffens, Upton Sinclair and Ray Stannard Baker. Tarbell's "History of the Standard Oil

Company" (1904) was a meticulously-documented and searing expose of ruthless competitive business practices and misuse of natural resources. It helped lead to anti-monopoly reforms and controls. Steffens' "Shame of the Cities," a series of magazine articles later published as a book, took a hard and revealing look at the pervasiveness of political and municipal corruption. As a reform writer, Baker turned out many articles on social and economic problems from a liberal standpoint. Upton Sinclair exposed wretched and filthy conditions in the meat packing industry.

In our own time, journalistic investigators like syndicated columnist Jack Anderson and reporters Seymour Hersh, Bob Woodward, Carl Bernstein, Donald Bartlett, James Steele, Morton Mintz and

"Given the time, effort and imagination it is possible for an amateur sleuth to get beneath surface appearances."

Clark Mollenhoff have set high standards for others to follow. The Woodward-Bernstein Watergate revelations led to President Nixon's downfall and resignation from office.

There are scores of other reporters, at both large and small newspapers, who are ferreting out corruption and wrongdoing in public office and the business world or exposing threats to health and safety, whether by hidden toxic chemicals or radioactive waste.

The average person may lack the background or depth of experience to achieve similar results.

But that should not preclude him or her from successfully tackling projects that merit investigation. Given the time, effort and imagination, it is possible for an amateur sleuth to get beneath surface appearance and unearth the truth about what really has happened or is happening.

You can do it, if you set your mind to it.

Investigators—whether reporters, police or private detectives—come in different sizes, shapes and temperament. Some are quiet spoken and methodical. Others may seem unduly aggressive, disorganized and tending to "fly by the seat of their pants." But often there are traits common to most of them.

To many observers, the investigative mind is characterized by relentless curiosity, skepticism and a willingness to follow where the facts lead. Like the great fictional detectives, it is challenged by a seemingly unfathomable puzzle. It gathers in gossip, trivia, facts, impressions and leads and tries to make sense of them.

All of us have our built-in biases and prejudices which we bring to any problems we are trying to solve. We have to learn to set these aside, or at least be aware of them. We have to learn how to be stubborn—refusing to give up when things don't come easily. Most of all, we have to learn to think.

If you have a problem or project you want to investigate, you should take a hard look at it first from a personal level.

Try to itemize what motives might account for a person's or company's behavior and actions. Using your own value system or conscience, think of every motive that might help explain the situation.

Then put yourself in the place of others who have different sets of value. Figure out what their motives might be and list these also. Make a written or mental record of every conceivable motive that might be involved, again regardless of how far-fetched or absurd they may seem.

The skeptical mind tries to weigh all possibilities. If we refuse to take this approach at the outset, we may miss the one avenue that explains the reason for what is happening.

Most of us have seen transparent cubes for displaying photographs. We should use our minds like these six-sided cubes.

Think of each cube side as a separate and distinct way of looking at or explaining things. We view one side and say this is how we explain a situation or motive. In our mind, we turn the cube so that we are looking at another side. We then think of another explanation, motive or set of circumstances. We turn the cube over repeatedly in our hands and minds—each time exploring a different approach or evaluation.

In searching for clues that might help us get at the information we need, we do the same mental exercise. Then it is up to us to check out each lead and assumption to the best of our ability. Sometimes the least-suspected motive or method gives us the answer. Hercule Poirot, Agatha Christie's revered sleuth, boasted of his "grey cells" in solving mysteries.

We have our photo cubes. With a little luck and hard work they should be enough.

Later, we will examine some specific investigative projects to see how this applies.

Often your success as an investigator will depend on your willingness to pit your intellect, instincts and perseverance against those of your opponent.

It is, at heart, a game of wits. If you suspect a person may be ripping off you, your family or community then you must attempt to put yourself in the position of that person. You try to think as he or she might think. If you were in his place, how would you pull off a scheme to enrich yourself at someone else's expense?

What steps might he have taken to succeed in his scheme? How did he expect to get away with it?

What might he have done to cover his tracks? How would you have done it? Did he make any mistakes or leave clues that could be traced? Did he do things that might have generated records or documents that you could check? What about people he dealt with? Are there any weak links—people whom you might get to talk about it?

Unraveling the answers can make such a game of wits a fascinating process. It may take a lot of hard and tedious work, often fraught with frustration. But the moments when you know you have put together critical pieces of the puzzle can be truly exhilarating and make it worth all the time and effort.

Because much of investigative work is a game of wits, it generally pays to "keep your cool" when you are trying to get at information or data that someone is eager to conceal. If you allow your passions or emotions to get out of control, you may well risk missing some important clue or connections that you might otherwise have spotted.

We previously mentioned the names of some outstanding investigative reporters. There are scores of others, however, who have won the admiration of their peers, and whose efforts often have led to major shake-ups in local or state government or have helped inform and protect the public against lurking evils or dangers. Sometimes the opponent is ignorance.

To some degree, all reporters and writers who do in-depth studies of topics that are important to our health, finances and welfare are engaging in investigative reporting. So too is the researcher who probes the past or present for historical pieces, profiles, analytical articles or books.

Hopefully, this publication may prove of some value to such persons.

There is, however, usually one characteristic that distinguishes investigative reporting or the truly investigative project from other types of research. Perhaps the best definition of investigative reporting is that it involves seeking to uncover information that has been deliberately concealed from public view. Sometimes, it is a matter of bringing together data never before assembled.

You may ask yourself: How can I expect to succeed, when I don't have the experience or background of a Jack Anderson, Seymour Hersh, Clark R. Mollenhoff or Jonathan Kwitny? There may be little likelihood that you can match their skills or success. But that doesn't mean that you are doomed to failure. You frequently can succeed if you set realistic goals for yourself and are willing to devote the time, talent and effort to investigating what is important to you.

All of us—regardless of whether we are office clerks, housewives, laborers, businessmen, civil servants or students—already share or can develop important investigative traits.

"Most of us enjoy gossip or rumors, although we may like to think ourselves above that sort of thing."

Our instincts often give us silent tips when there is something peculiar about a deal, whether it be a bargain purchase, real estate transaction or an unusual governmental action.

Most of us enjoy gossip or rumors, although we may like to think ourselves above that sort of thing. Our minds, however, have a way of storing away such tidbits.

The investigative person learns to be a good listener. Sometimes a meaningless tidbit or absurd rumor can provide a valuable insight and may prove worth checking out. You treat all rumors as being unsubstantiated, unless and until you can prove otherwise.

Being a good listener is important when you are trying to uncover information. Often a gentle question can turn the conversation in the direction you want, without your being too obvious.

If you find that a source or person shares your suspicions about some officials, agencies or companies, the best approach often is to confide that you share similar feelings or views. He may already know, or be in a position to find, information that would be useful to you. You have to be wary at times, and ask yourself whether he would be likely to tip off the party you want to investigate.

There are times when you can get a disgruntled or disenchanted "insider" to confide in you by appealing to what motivates that person.

The successful trigger may be that person's desire to avenge some slight. Or it could be an appeal to his or her moral code. Sometimes even the most loyal employee will feel compelled to speak out against actions of their company or associates when it offends their sense of what is right and proper.

Public Records Can Sketch A Remarkably Clear Portrait

THERE are no formulas that will guarantee success in every investgative project. Each problem or project differs to some degree. But I have three favorite lines that sum up what I believe is a sound and basic approach. They add up to a total of five words. Their value has been proven time and time again in my own experience.

Think

Think Activity

Think Again

The word — activity — as used here means an action or function. It is a key element in what I have sought to describe as an on-going mental gymnastics approach toward investigative problem solving. Almost all human activities produce a trail of records that frequently can be followed by the discerning investigator, whether he or she is an expert or the most untutored amateur.

"Think. Think Activity. Think Again."

Remember the fictional John Gregory Simonds, who in the darkness told us only his name and home community? I said that even though we were given only such scant information, we could in most cases be able to "recreate" him and learn almost everything about him without meeting him personally. How can it be done? The answer is simply that we use our minds. And the five-word formula: Think/Think Activity/Think Again.

How does that apply here?

Consider what actions or activities were involved in John Gregory Simond's briefly glimpsed appearance in the auditorium and what records or

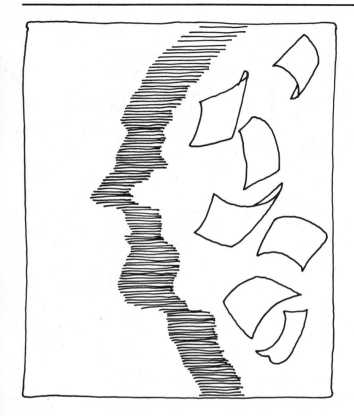

documents were generated by these actual or implied activities.

What questions might naturally arise from his appearance before you? One question is how did he get there? He could have walked there, of course. But because we no longer live under wilderness conditions and therefore lack the finely-honed senses and skills needed in following someone's tracks, it is extremely unlikely that his act of walking would have produced any record or physical evidence we could examine.

He could have come by bicycle. But here again, there is little, if anything, that would be useful to us. If we knew what Simonds looked like, and what clothes he was wearing, we might try to find someone who saw such a person arriving on foot or by bike.

Let us suppose, however, that Simonds drove to the building. If he came by car, this opens up two possible avenues of records. One would be his driver's license. The second would be car registration data. Either or both of these sources could help shed considerable light on our subject.

In many states, driver licenses are issued and handled either by the Secretary of State's office or the state's Motor Vehicle Registry. The latter quite often is a division within a state Revenue Department. Driver licenses are public records in many states. You have only to reach into your wallet or purse examine your own license to realize what a wealth of information is there.

Chances are it would list your date of birth, address, age, weight, height, the color of your hair and eyes, and whether you are required to wear glasses while driving. It also might include a photo of you. There also is an excellent chance it would list your Social Security number, and perhaps indicate whether you are willing, upon death, to allow use of certain organs for surgical transplants.

If we were to obtain a copy of Simonds' driver's license, it would help us to form a mental image of him. It might also give us a clue about his driving habits. He may be an excellent driver with an unblemished record. But on the other hand, he may have compiled a poor driving record marred by numerous traffic violations. His license may have been suspended or revoked at some time, possibly in connection with some court proceedings we could examine. It is often possible to find out what kind of a driving record a person has from a state agency or from other sources.

"You have only to examine your driver's license to realize what a wealth of information is there."

Some states consider driver licenses are public records. Others allow access to them only by law enforcement agencies.

In Missouri, for example, driver licenses and vehicle registration records are public records. Anyone can ask for copies of these records or data on anyone, without asking the other person's permission or even knowing him or her.

License and registration data can be obtained on formal request by letter. Write to the Missouri

Department of Revenue, Jefferson State Office Building, Jefferson City, Mo. 65101. Send driver license inquiries to the above address, attention: Driver License Bureau. Vehicle registration inquiries should be directed to: Motor Vehicle Bureau.

At this writing, there is a $1 charge for each driver license or registration record requested.

In the case of a vehicle registration, regardless of the state involved, you must provide the license plate number of the vehicle you want checked. It also would be good if you included in your request any information you might have about the year, make and model of the vehicle. This also could be used to double-check the data you get back from the state. The state's reply will include the name of the listed owner, that person or firm's address, and the year, make and model of the vehicle.

In Missouri, driver license data that can be obtained from the state on written request includes the driver's name, address, date of birth, height, weight, color of eyes and hair, and any special driving restrictions, such as a requirement that the driver wear eyeglasses. The information would include whether it is a regular driving permit or a chauffeur's license, the license expiration date, as well as any notations relating to suspension or revocation of driving privileges.

When requesting driver license data, you should provide the state agency involved with at least the driver's full name and last known addresss. If possible, also include the driver's date of birth, or approximate age, and Social Security number.

In New York State, driving records, license applications or renewals, and vehicle registrations are also public records. You can get copies of these records on written request to the New York State Department of Motor Vehicles, Empire State Plaza, Albany, N.Y. 12228.

Request relating to driving license applications and renewals should be directed to the department's Public Service Bureau. There is a $3 fee for each request, plus 50 cents if you want the copy certified. The license copy includes the applicant's age, date of birth, height, weight and color of hair and eyes.

For a $2.50 fee, also directed to the department's Public Service Bureau, you can obtain a copy of any

New York state motorist's driving record. It lists any traffic violations the driver was convicted of over the

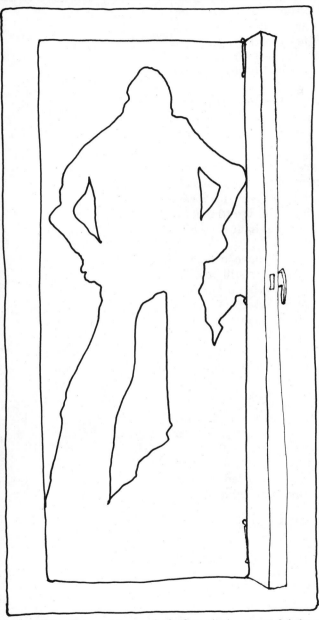

preceding three-year period. Convictions on driving-while-intoxicated charges remain on the record for 10 years.

Written requests for vehicle registration data

should be sent to the attention of the New York Department of Motor Vehicles' Public Request Bureau, at the address noted earlier. There is a $2 fee for each such request. If you are planning to submit numerous requests, you might ask the agency to forward you MV-15 registration request forms.

A number of states will not provide this kind of information to private citizens.

Let us return again to our Mr. Simonds. If he had driven to the auditorium building, there is a good chance that he owned the vehicle he used to get there.

Let us assume that we learned from the state that Simonds was listed as owner of a 1980 Lincoln Continental, a 1979 Jaguar and a 1980 recreation van. This indicates perhaps that Simonds is affluent. It would certainly cast him in a different light than if he owned only a 1965 Volkswagen Bug.

If in your state, citizens do not have access to license and vehicle registration data, it is still possible to find out from other sources. Perhaps you can locate a friendly contact in the Secretary of State's office or the state's Motor Vehicles Registry. There are also other avenues.

Many of us are acquainted with someone in our local police department or sheriff's offices. Police can easily obtain this information and do so almost instantaneously through computer checks.

For example, when a police car stops a speeding vehicle, the officer often will remain in his patrol car while he radios in a license check. This is normally done for two reasons. One, he wants to determine whether the vehicle has been reported stolen. Second, it enables him to find out who is the registered owner of the vehicle.

A citizen at times can persuade a member of his or her community's police force to get a license "rundown" by explaining why it is needed. Another possibility is to ask a newspaper reporter who covers local police as part of his regular news beat to obtain the information.

Sometimes you have to search out someone who has a police, reporter or political friend. Your alderman, county prosecutor, state legislator, county council member or even your ward committeeman or committeewoman might be able to help you get the information.

Data about car ownership and registration frequently can be obtained if you have a friend or contact in the county or city assessor's office. The county assessor generally needs access to vehicle ownership records so he can bill taxpayers for personal property taxes on cars and other vehicles they own. A good way to size up your prospects here

"Bureaucracies can be a curse, but also a blessing."

might be to ask an employee in the county assessor's office to check your own vehicle registration. Some people with flexible ethical standards have been known to ask about a fictitious brother or sister's record.

Earlier we said bureaucracies can be a curse, but also a blessing. So, too, here.

Depending on the size of your town or county, the taxing and collection process may be vested in more than one office. Often the official who assesses taxes — the person who determines how much taxes are owed — is not the official who collects them. Thus, your community or county may have a collector's office, with its own files or records on vehicle ownership.

Let us return to our fictitious John Gregory Simonds, from suburban Webster Groves in St. Louis County, and look through another side of the transparent photo cube. He arrived at the auditorium, we know. What follows? He may have come directly from his work or job. There would be records associated with this. Or, he may have come from his home.

It is possible for us to find out where he lives and examine records related to his residency. If he is an apartment dweller, we can learn how desirable the location appears to be and what the likely rental or leasing costs are for such an apartment.

If Simonds is a homeowner, this generates a

volume of records. We can discover, for example, where Simonds' home is, when he purchased it, from whom, its value — at least for tax purposes — and perhaps the price he paid for it. We could go see the home, and from real estate agents get a good idea how much homes of similar size and features are selling for in that area. We probably could determine whether he obtained a mortgage on the property, the name of the lending institution, the duration of the loan and its annual interest.

At the same time, we ought to be able to compile a listing of all properties Simonds owns, if any, in a given city or county.

These records relating to property and home ownership generally are found in the county or city Recorder of Deeds' office and are open to public inspection. By examining records in the city or county assessor's office, we could find out what the taxes on the home are and whether they have been paid or are delinquent. All of this information is part of the public record and readily accessible.

"Almost everything a person does produces some record or trail. Let us consider our own lives for clues."

What we are doing is building a profile of our Mr. Simonds.

Similarly, we can build a profile on almost any person — whether he or she is a public official, a friend, a neighbor, a business associate, or a business competitor. We can do it usually with a good deal of thoroughness and entirely within the law.

We said earlier that almost everything a person does produces some record or trail. Let us consider our own lives for insights and clues.

What would be more logical than to start at the beginning? The moment we are born, we set the stage for our first record — our birth certificate. Later, as we grow older, we attend school. This produces report cards, attendance reports, class photos, scrapbooks, club and team rosters, school yearbooks and news items in school publications.

We check out books at the library. More records. We make purchases; still more records. We graduate and there are diplomas and degrees. We get married, buy a house and have children. Sometimes we get divorced.

The list of things we do is almost endless and so is the trail of records we generate. Finally, we die. There is the death certificate and a tombstone to mark our grave site. But it doesn't necessarily stop there. There may be a will, probate court proceedings and a legal battle among our heirs.

A BUSINESS enterprise or company can often be traced through its life span much as we would track a human. People and companies share many of the same life stages. Each is born. But instead of a birth certificate, a business may come into being with the filing of articles of incorporation, usually with the Secretary of State's office.

Like our report cards or birthday cards marking passage of years, business firms often are required to file annual reports with the state. These reports list the names of the officers and directors of the company, and whether there have been any changes in their ranks in the preceding year. Like people, a business can die. The death, or bankruptcy, of a firm often is reflected in articles of dissolution.

We will go into greater detail about learning about corporations, their assets and secrets later on.

Let us here return again to John Gregory Simonds, keeping in mind that he could be any person — a friend, stranger or enemy.

From a variety of sources, we may be able to learn his address. We have already cited driver's license and automobile registration data. Often we have to do no more than opening up the telephone directory.

One of the most valuable sources of information is a directory that lists the names and addresses of persons who reside in specific communities. There are directories published for many, if not most, cities in the United States. One such publisher is the R. L. Polk & Co., which prepares and publishes more than 1400 city and suburban directories.

The Polk Directory is put out each year and lists in alphabetical order the names of all adult residents of a given community, as well as an alphabetical listing of business and professional concerns. But the Polk Directory also gives us additional valuable information.

For example, it generally lists a person's street address and community, where the person is employed or his occupation, and the person's marital status, including the name of his or her spouse.

"Often you can see a directory for your area at the public library, police department or assessor's."

Polk's directory also offers two other valuable sections. One is a street and avenue guide, featuring an alphabetical listing of streets names. Addresses are listed numerically, with the name of the resident appearing beside each specific address. Another valuable section is a numerical telephone directory, showing who has each number.

Polk maintains directory libraries in many cities and towns throughout the United States and Canada where the public can examine directories. Often you can see a directory for your area at the public library, police department or city or county assessor's office. You can write to the main office of R. L. Polk & Co., Publishers, 6400 Monroe Boulevard, Box 500, Taylor, Michigan, 48180, or telephone (313) 292-3200.

There are other publishers of directories that provide valuable information.

Cole Publications, for example, publishes more than 150 criss-cross reference directories that have two sections each. One section is an alphabetical listing of street names, with the addresses in numerical order. Next to each address is listed the name of the resident and his or her telephone number. The other section lists telephone numbers numerically, giving the phone subscriber's name and address.

Areas served by Cole include Manhattan and other New York City buroughs and communities in such states as Texas, Pennsylvania, Louisiana, Colorado, Washington, Oregon, Idaho, Tennessee, Minnesota, North and South Dakota, Kansas and

Missouri. The directories are both sold and leased.

Cole Publication's main office is at 901 West Bond Street, Lincoln, Nebraska, 68521, telephone (402) 475-4591.

Because many directories, like Polk's, are published on an annual basis, it means that we can check directories over a period of years to see what changes have occurred in a specific listing.

We could run a check on a person — say our Mr. John Gregory Simonds, for one year, two years or even 10 or 20 years or more, if conditions and circumstances warrant. We should be able to tell

whether Simonds' address, occupation and marital status have changed over the years.

Let us assume that we check a 1979 suburban directory for St. Louis County and find this hypothetical listing:

Simonds, John G., and Susan J., h782 Wing Drive,
    Webster Groves, eng Fortune Co.

This entry tells you that Simonds' wife's name is Susan, that he lives at 782 Wing Drive in Webster Groves and works as an engineer at Fortune Co. Let us pretend that we examine the earlier editions of this directory dating back 15 years and that we find the following entries on Simonds:

1977-78 directory:
Simonds, John Gregory & Susan, h782 Wing
    Drive, Webster Groves, sales mgr Fortune Co.

1976-77 directory:
Simonds, John G. and Susan J. h582 *Delaney
    Lane, University City,* sales mgr Fortune Co.

1975 directory:
Simonds, John G. and Susan, h 582 Delaney Lane,
University City, *salesman, Premier Beer Co.*

1970 directory:
Simonds, John G. and Susan, *218 Murphy Lane,*
Webster Groves, salesman, *Atlas Products Co.*

1968 directory:
Simonds, John Gregory and *Anita, 815
Presidential Drive,* Webster Groves, salesman
Atlas Products Co.

In the listings, I have italicized changes in the directory entries over the years examined. The entries indicate that Simonds has changed his residence several times and has changed jobs. Also the listing reflects a change in his marital status. In the 1968 directory his wife's first name was listed as Anita. Two years later, his wife's name is listed as Susan. Thus it would appear that sometime around or after 1968, he and Anita were divorced or perhaps Anita died.

The acts of divorce and death each produce records. If there was a divorce, the documents and files relating to the divorce proceeding would be filed with the county circuit court and would be public record. If the divorce was a contested one the records might include detailed information about the couple's finances and the distribution of their property when the marriage was dissolved. In such instances, sometimes even copies of a person's income tax returns find their way into the divorce records.

If Anita had died, there would be a death certificate and perhaps an obituary in a local newspaper. Such obituaries often can be a valuable source of information about the deceased, giving family background, previous employment and civic activities.

Your newspaper may allow you to look through back copies if you give a valid reason and know the approximate date of the event. Public libraries usually microfilm files of their local newspapers dating back years.

An obituary and a death certificate are not always the final records of a person's life. After a person dies, there is often a will to be probated and an estate to be settled. County probate courts generally are the arena of such records.

One need only know the name of the deceased person to obtain the probate records. These records frequently provide detailed information about the property and financial holdings of the deceased and how the estate is to be distributed.

As in life, the government, when someone dies, continues to insist on its share of the estate. There often are estate taxes to be paid both at the state and federal level and this information will be a matter of probate record.

In the case of John Gregory Simonds, the directory entries we extracted also list his occupation and employers.

For more information about Simonds, we could contact the companies he worked for and talk to his employers and co-workers. His former co-workers might be excellent sources of information about what kind of man he was when they knew him — his traits and work habits. We might also learn the names of customers he served as a salesman and then interview them.

However, the directory entries could also lead us to other potential important sources — his present and former neighbors.

For each of the years we are interested in, we could check Simonds' home address and then go to the street guide section of the directory. There it would list addresses of all the homes or buildings on his block, the names of the persons living there at the time the directory was compiled and even their telephone numbers in many cases.

'Other potential important sources are present and former neighbors.''

Thus we could build a listing of most persons who were his neighbors over the years and then seek to interview them. If a former neighbor has moved to a new address, we might be able to find that person in the current directory.

This approach is just as valid, whether we are trying to uncover information about Simonds or some obscure poet, musician, a missing relative, lost heir, or political figure who may have lived in a particular community or city several decades ago and then vanished. It might still be possible to track down the neighbors and people who knew our missing person.

Interviews with these former neighbors could provide a lot of background information on the subject being investigated or researched.

They could help us build a profile of what type person the subject was — whether he was law-abiding or frequently in trouble with neighbors and the authorities. They could tell us where he worked, tell us about his temperament, his friends and associates, and his family life.

Thus Does the Earth, and Its Records, Endureth Forever

PERHAPS you have driven down a tree-lined street and wondered who owned a particularly attractive home. Or perhaps you have done business in some plush office of a building that you thought might have been owned by a company you have been dealing with.

The following section is intended to help you find out as much as possible about who owns what in real estate.

It is designed to help you uncover the history of a specific home, building, estate or a block. You should be able to learn who owns it, how long they have had it, from whom they acquired it, whether they are delinquent on any taxes on the property, and whether they obtained financing when they bought it, and from what bank or institution they borrowed to acquire the property.

Once, several centuries ago, man was convinced that the earth was flat. He knew this to be a fact. And rightly so.

But then along came the scientists and the historians' and they began to deflate this myth. Let me now offer some other truisms that will help any person who wants to learn about property ownership:

1. Land is forever with us.
2. The entire world is divided into "city blocks."
3. The world consists of givers and getters.

You say it's silly to believe the earth is flat. But for our purposes, it is wise to accept that as a truism. It will help you understand how to investigate the history of real estate transactions and to unravel them so they will be as clear as a puzzle that has been assembled piece by piece.

We ought to consider the earth as one vast expanse of land. To put it another way, we should think of earth as a huge map laid out on some enormous table. The map is flat. But it depicts the location and boundaries of the continents, the ocean, and the nations and territories. A map of wilderness

35

might show us the characteristics of the land, the layout of the land, and rivers and other natural phenomena. Or, a city map might show us the layout of a city divided into city blocks.

It would help us if we would consider the world not only to be flat, but simply to be one huge map like a city divided into blocks.

When I speak of blocks, that could refer to blocks that are square or rectangular. But just as likely, the city blocks may be octagonal or crescent shaped or a variety of geometric patterns. In each instance, however, the city block depicts a specific parcel of land.

We all know what a regular city block looks like.

One such block might consist of twenty homes. Another might have 30, 40 or even 50 homes. Still another might have as few as six or 10. But each one has a certain number of home lots, each with a specific size and dimension. We might, for example, find that in one block a lot might have a 60 foot frontage and a depth of 125 feet. In another block, the homes might be built on one, two or even three-acre lots. In this case, we might refer to the city blocks as subdivisions. But in each instance, the location and the boundaries of each specific lot are parts of records that are open to the public.

There are several reasons why we have emphasized that land is forever. Buildings come and go, but the land beneath them remains.

We have all read accounts of buildings being razed to make room for new high-rises. We have read accounts of whole building projects, like the huge Pruitt-Igoe public housing project in St. Louis, for instance, being leveled. But each time, the land remains. Not only is the land permanent, but the

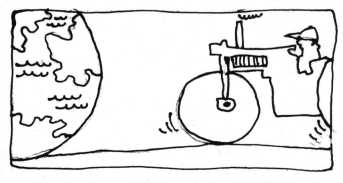

record of the land is permanent. It is easy to understand why.

Many of us, during our school days, may have been exposed to the theory of territorial imperative. This holds, roughly, that an animal stakes out a portion of land and defends that area. The animal views a certain area as his own, to be defended at all costs.

Man, in much the same manner, over the centuries, has battled to acquire and defend the land. We have had wars, tribal fights and unending conflicts over who is to own what land.

"The world is made up of givers and getters. These are two broad but all-inclusive categories."

Even in our more civilized periods, disputes often arise as to exactly what property is owned by which person.

If there were not records that could be checked showing the exact boundaries and ownership of property, our society would be plunged into far more disputes than we have even now.

Thus, records are an essential feature of protecting ownership rights. The records can be traced back for decades, often for centuries.

In real estate, the world is made up of givers and getters. These are two broad, but all-inclusive, categories.

The givers are persons, firms or institutions that own property and convey it to another party. They may sell the property to another person, trade it, will it or bequeath it. Or they may donate it for some charitable or family purpose.

The getters are those who receive property, whether it be conveyed to them through sale, trade or inheritance.

In public records, which document virtually all property transactions, the givers frequently are known by a more formal name, grantors. Thus the book showing who conveyed property for a given year generally is referred to as the grantor book. In another location, the names of persons conveying

37

property may be listed in a book referred to as the direct index.

Conversely, the person who receives the property is called the grantee and his name is listed in alphabetical order in the grantee book. Depending on your community or county, the grantee book may be called the indirect index or the inverted index.

ALTHOUGH practices vary from area to area throughout our nation, real estate transactions are usually recorded or grouped on an annual basis. That is, the names of all persons or parties conveying property in a given year are found in a specific book or volume for that year. Similarly, the names of property recipients usually are incorporated into one volume, often referred to as the grantee index, the indirect index, reverse index or the inverted index.

In some places these annual listings might not be in books, but instead might be on microfilm or a computer printout. But the same principle normally applies: real estate transactions are filed and recorded as they occur, but then are grouped together for a given year.

How are these grantor (giver) and grantee (getter) books arranged? They are most frequently arranged first alphabetically by last name of the person conveying or receiving the property, and then chronologically according to the dates the documents were filed.

Thus, all persons whose last name begins with an "A" are grouped under the letter A in alphabetical order.

If, because of a community or county's size, there is a massive volume of transactions or a particularly large number of persons whose names begin with a specific letter of the alphabet, then frequently the listing under that letter will be subdivided into smaller groups. Thus the first grouping might run from Ae through Am, followed by units covering An through Ap and Aq through Az.

Where are such real estate records kept?

Throughout much of the United States, they are on file at the Recorder of Deeds' office in the county, city or municipality where the property is located. The records invariably are open to public view. And they are easily understood, once you have mastered some of the principles involved.

It is generally easy to obtain copies of the documents, although in most instances a fee will be charged for such copies.

Real estate transactions are recorded daily in alphabetical order as they occur. In most political subdivisions the daily records are then compiled into one volume or set of volumes after the year ends.

Let us take a look at a segment of a typical but hypothetical page from a grantor's index:

Typical Grantor's Page

Filing Date	Grantor	Grantee	Type of Instrument	Daily Number	Date of Instrument	Book	Page	Description	Consideration
2-5-80	Allen, Michael A. et ux	United Federal Savings & Loan	DT	217	2-1-80	3867	292	C. B. 6218 Main Chatsworth Addn	$38,000
2-5-80	Alden, James C. and Clara F.	Santone, August and Sarina G.	QC	115	2-4-80	3867	310	Lot 82, Boswell Subdivision, Sect. 2	$1
2-5-80	Alway, Jane L.	Rodenbecker, Gray F.	WD	105	2-4-80	3867	378	C. B. 2120 Maiden Ln Walnut Hgts. Addn	$1
2-7-80	Almon, Anthony J. et ux	Franklin, Agnes F.	part. Rel.	89	2-5-80	3867	410	Lots 17, 18 Agawam Hunt Subd, Addn 3	Book/Page 2754/ 310
2-7-80	Allen, Daniel T, et ux	Summers, Anthony et ux	WD	134	2-3-80	3868	32	C. B. 4203 Marcus 55 ft. x 132 ft., 6 in. Senhauer Addn, Lot 54	$1
2-8-80	Alliance Federal Savings & Loan	Renshaw, William T. et ux	rel.	219	2-8-80	3868	304	Lot 79, Antonio Subdivision, Walnut Hills	Book/Page 2251/ 542
2-8-80	Allen, Michael A. et ux	United Federal Savings & Loan	DT	119	2-8-80	3868	620	Chatterly Estates Lots 3-6, 2nd Addn.	$67,000
2-8-80	Aldridge, John J. et ux	Brazie, Josephine C.	WD	97	2-6-80	3869	211	Amberdeen Gardens Lot 18, Spanner Addn.	$1 Book/Page
2-8-80	Altoona Credit Union	Simpson, Gerald P. and Kathleen	rel.	187	2-1-80	3870	99	C. B. 2130, Helena Lane 72 ft. 11 in/irreg School Section 16 Addn.	1874/ 319
2-11-80	Allen, Michael A.	Roche, Lewis T.	QC	59	2-8-80	3870	345	C. B. 6087 Newport 120 ft. x 170 ft. Carson Hgts. Addn.	$1
2-11-80	Aldani, Michele	Aldani, Roberta	WD	197	2-8-80	3871	243	Canterbury Subdivision Lots 3 and 4, 3rd Addn. Santiago Estates	$1
2-12-80	Allen, LeRoy et ux	Carlton, Walter A., et al	WD	237	2-11-80	3871	521	Santiago Estates Lots 3, 5, 7, First Phase	$1

It is obvious from the sample page that the listing here is both alphabetical and chronological. This means that if you or I wanted to check out one specific person we would have to plow through every entry in the AL letter grouping for an entire year to pinpoint any transactions that year involving a person named Allard.

In other cities or counties the task might be much easier. This would be particularly true if, at year's end, the records were correlated strictly on an alphabetical basis. This is done in many political subdivisions.

Let us take a column-by-column look at our sample page.

DATE — Refers to the date the instrument involved was filed and recorded. Normally, deeds and other documents are filed within a few days after they are signed and executed. But this is not always the case. Sometimes there will be delays of weeks or months between the time deeds are executed and filed. It could even be one or two years or more.

And there are occasions when deeds are executed but never filed. This is a frequent device that is used if one person wants to keep his or her interest in a property off the public record.

Companies or persons who wish to conceal their ownership or interest in property often resort to use of "straw parties" or dummy corporations set up for that specific purpose. A straw party usually is a person, who, although listed as a titleholder, actually has no real involvement or ownership interest in the transaction. (More on straw parties later and how you can often find out whom they are fronting for.)

There can be many legitimate reasons for delays in filing. But sometimes they seem to be self-explanatory.

In one Missouri suburban county, the developers who wanted to build luxurious lake-front residences took an option to buy a tract of land at the proposed site from the owner — who just happened to be a member of the county's zoning commission. The developer paid for the option, and offered a handsome per-acre price for the property.

The option agreement was executed two weeks before a crucial zoning change was granted to the developers, with the board member voting for the rezoning.

But it was not filed until nearly 18 months later. Thus there was no public notice of the option or any relationship it might have had to the timing of the rezoning.

As it happened, a few weeks after the option was filed, I was assigned as a reporter to set up a news bureau in that same county. During a routine check of property transactions involving all county officials, I chanced across the option.

The minutes of the meeting contained nothing to indicate that he had informed fellow board members of the option agreement between him and the developers. My check of the zoning records also disclosed instances of conflicts of interest involving other board members. Rather than keeping things under wraps, the option filing delay had led to a series of detailed disclosures involving zoning board members.

"Rather than keeping things under wraps, the filing delay led to a series of disclosures."

GRANTOR — this column shows the name of the person, firm or institution conveying property, rights or interest to another person or party. The grant may involve title to property, but it could also be an easement or a promise to repay a loan or mortgage. In the case of individuals, the grantor is listed according to last name. Businesses and institutions are listed alphabetically by the first word in their title. Thus, the Alpha Contracting Co. would appear under the letter A. Some political subdivisions maintain separate listings for corporate entities.

TYPE OF INSTRUMENT — the column heading explains itself. It may simply read: "Instrument." Letter codes are generally used to reflect the nature of the document or transaction being filed. For the most part, title to property is conveyed or transferred through a warranty deed (WD) or a quit-claim deed (QC).

In a general warranty deed, the party conveying a property pledges to warrant and defend the title against all claims. A quit claim deed merely conveys whatever interest a person may hold in the property, but does not warrant and defend against any claims.

Our sample page from the grantor's book includes a number of other shorthand codes. DT stands for deed of trust. This, in effect, is a written promise to pay off a mortgage, loan or promissory note. The deed usually sets forth the amount borrowed, the duration of the loan and the repayment schedule. At times, this information is not included and instead is alluded to as being in a separate but unfiled document.

In our sampling, "part. rel." refers to a partial release of title or other rights that may have been conveyed in connection with a mortgage or promissory note.

For example, let's say we borrow $40,000 from a bank so that we can buy four one-acre house lots. To protect itself, the bank stipulates that if we default on our payments it can take over the title and control of the property. The agreement may also provide that for each $10,000 that we pay off on the loan, the bank will relinquish any claim to one lot. If we repay

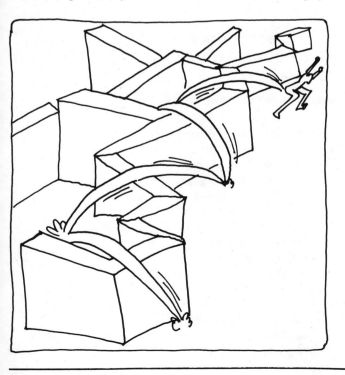

$20,000, it would be required to release two of the four lots, for example.

Easement deeds or agreements invariably are filed in county or city real estate records. Similarily so are agreements relating to oil and mineral rights. Other types of deeds include trustee deeds, administrator deeds, executor deeds and sheriff's deeds.

RELEASE — generally alludes to a full release by the lender on completion of repayment of the mortgage or loan.

DAILY NUMBER — a number assigned to a deed by the recorder's office when the document is filed. It is used to help expedite locating documents.

DATE OF INSTRUMENT — the date a document was signed and executed.

BOOK/PAGE — the number of the book and page where a copy of a deed or other document appears. It may be in a bound volume or on microfilm.

DESCRIPTION — usually a brief legal description of the property involved in a transaction. A detailed description appears on the deed. Often it is both desirable and necessary to use the deed description to avoid confusion and error.

"In some states and areas, records will disclose the price that an owner paid for property."

CONSIDERATION — an exchange of things of value. Often the dollar amount in this column reflects a legal contractual minimum, rather than listing what was paid for a property. In the case of deeds of trust, it usually lists the amount of the loan or mortgage. Where a release or partial release is being made, it often merely lists the book and page number where the original deed of trust is recorded.

In some states and areas, records will disclose the price that an owner paid for property. But in other states, such as Missouri, neither the buyer nor the seller is required to disclose that information.

Yet it is possible in such non-disclosure states to get a good line on the actual price in cases where property was conveyed during the roughly two-decade period prior to 1967. By law, during this period, federal tax stamps were required to be affixed to such deeds.

The stamps indicated the purchase price to the nearest $500 or $1,000.

Each $1.10 of the face amount of the federal stamps represented $1,000 of the sales price. Each 55-cent stamp reflected $500. Thus is the stamps totaled $33, the indicated sales price was about $33,000. If $33.55 in stamps were affixed to the deed, it would have meant a sales price of about $33,500.

There was an exception, however, whereby stamps were not required for any part of the sale price that involved assumption of an existing mortgage. Let's say, for example, that a buyer agreed to assume a $10,000 mortgage and to pay the seller an additional $20,000 for a home. In such a case, the actual sale price would have been $30,000, but the federal tax stamps would have reflected only $20,000 of that amount.

The indirect index is arranged in exactly the same manner as the direct or grantor index, except that in the first column, are the names of the recipients of property.

If we examine the sample grantor page, we might note that Michael A. Allen was involved in three separate transactions — two deeds of trust and one quit-claim deed — during the month of February, 1980.

Should we choose to, we might well be able to trace all real estate dealings involving Allen in a given county or city over a period of years. This could be done much the same as we would track a person through criss-cross (city) directories over the years.

It would involve checking both the grantor and grantee books, year by year, and finding each transaction in which the person we are interested in was a party. We could go back 10, 20 or even more years. And we could check records relating to that person's spouse, family and other relatives.

To get a complete picture, we would have to examine both the grantor and grantee indexes. If we were to check just one type of index, we might miss some valuable information. At the end of our study, we would have a chronological listing of all properties that an individual or company acquired from someone or conveyed to someone.

It is possible and even likely that a person can be both a giver and getter in relation to one single transaction.

For example, when you or I purchased our home, we were a grantee. We received the property from someone. But if you are like most Americans, you undoubtedly did not pay cash for your home. More likely, you had to obtain a mortgage of some type to help pay for the property. In return, you gave the lender the right to claim the property in the event you defaulted.

"Although there may be variations in different counties, the principles of record-keeping are similar."

When you signed the deed of trust or promissory note, you became a grantor and thus your name wound up in the direct index. Although the deed of trust would list the amount of the loan in almost all cases, this figure could be substantially less than the actual purchase price.

The unknown factor would be the size of the down payment made. That would not be part of the public record in most states.

The lay person interested in checking real estate transactions should remember that although there may be variations in record-keeping in different counties or states, the principles are remarkably similar. The language may vary, but it is a world of givers and getters, no matter where you live.

What is important is the process. One way to begin mastering the process is to start on familiar ground. If you or anyone in your family is a property owner, you could go to your county or city Recorder of Deeds and check these holdings.

We sometimes hear about callous and indifferent public employees who will scarcely lift a finger to help anyone. But based on my own experiences in checking an array of different types of records in scores of cities and counties in six states from the East Coast through the Midwest, this is an undeserved knock.

Most public employees are helpful, with many going out of their way to assist people in checking records maintained by their offices. Not only will the office employees involved help, but often it is possible to get guidance and assistance from title company personnel who are experts in examining real estate records and transactions. Often, title companies will be assigned space right in the Recorder of Deeds' offices. Their employees can be valuable allies in helping you analyze documents so as to avoid mistakes.

We have seen that we can trace an individual's or company's real estate transactions, both as a recipient and as a seller of property, for virtually any period we might desire.

Similarly, we could go to the county or city assessor's office and examine records there to determine what the tax assessments were on these properties for each year involved.

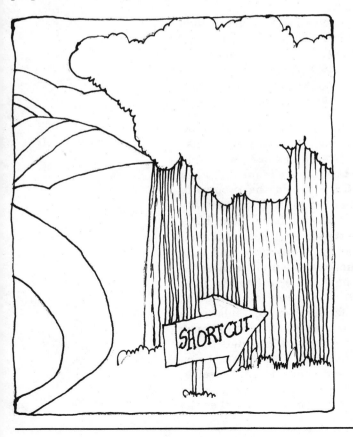

PROPERTY is normally assessed at a specific percentage of its purported real market value. But, in many areas of the nation, even within the same county or state, there can be a great disparity in assessments — and thus, also in taxes due. In the same county, you might find that although newer homes are assessed at a rate close to their true value, older homes might not have been assessed for 10 years or more. Thus the assessments would be comparatively low on these properties.

What happens in some areas is that when a builder puts up a home or commercial structure, the cost estimate set out in the building permit often may be used for assessing purposes. Or, perhaps the sales price is the figure used. In contrast to a new home, a house built 40 years ago right next door or down the block may have been last assessed one or two decades ago when homes were selling for one-third to one-half what they are going for now.

If you own a home you feel is assessed unduly high compared to others in your neighborhood, you could check your city or county assessment records for homes of roughly the same value in your general area. This might strengthen your argument that you are being asked to pay more in taxes than is equitable.

Just as you can trace the assessed value placed on a given property over a period of years, you can also trace the actual tax bill for each of those years. And you can see whether the taxes are delinquent or have been paid when due. If you are in the process of buying a home or other property, you can, by checking real estate records we have cited here, determine whether there are some tax liens or unpaid taxes outstanding against the property — and thus protect yourself in your negotiations and purchases.

Here is the kind of thing that can happen. Let's say a family hires a contractor to remodel a kitchen. Or, maybe, build a new family room or replace the roof or home siding. The homeowner fails to fully pay for the work done or materials used. He offers to sell the home and you agree to buy it, with the sale being handled completely between yourself and the seller. The seller gets his money.

Months pass and suddenly you discover that the

contractor who did remodeling or other work for the former owner is now demanding that you make good on the money still owed to him by the person you purchased the property from. He may tell you he has liens on the property.

Or, consider this. Let's imagine that the former owner paid the contractor the entire amount owed. But the contractor failed to pay his suppliers for lumber, roofing or other materials used at the home. Just as suddenly, you may find them insisting that you make good on the debts, even though you had no part in them.

If you purchase your home with a mortgage from a bank or other lending institution, they invariably will insist that a formal title search be made before letting the loan go through. An experienced title searcher will rarely miss detecting such liens.

There are times, however, when it may be important to you to do some checking on your own before you will want to incur expenses and waste time in negotiations on problem-plagued properties.

Depending on where you live, there frequently are short cuts that you can use in compiling an index or profile of the property holdings and transactions of a person or business.

One of the easiest ways is to go to the assessor's office and ask for a listing of all property held by a particular party or institution. If your subject is a person, you might want to get a listing of properties owned by his parents or other family members or relatives. Similarly, in the case of a conglomerate, you would do well to get a listing of its subsidiaries' holdings.

Often the assessor's office may include — either in its plat maps or assessing records — such data as the deed book and page on which the transaction can be found whereby the property was acquired. These, in turn, might list similar data involving previous owner acquisitions. Thus, it might be easy to check the history of a single property over a period of one or two decades.

We referred to plat maps. These are simply line drawings showing the location and boundaries of land parcels. They may just show the property lines. Or they may also sketch in the rough location and size of buildings on the property.

Property assessment records usually consist of sets of valuations: one for the land itself and the other for improvements there, usually meaning a home or building.

In rural areas, the land values may be set on a basis of a per-acre value estimate. In cities, it often is based on front footage or based on the square footage. Often, an assessed valuation is arrived at by whim.

Other factors that can enter the picture include family, friendship, political or business ties. Sometimes a few inexpensive gifts or campaign contributions are the real reasons for a low assessment. Every now and then, it simply is a case of a substantial under-the-table bribe. These are hard to detect because the payments usually are in cash and no receipts are given.

Let me include an important warning here. It may be easier in some areas to get a line on a person or corporation's property holdings by merely checking assessment records or the tax collector's records. But these often have a major loophole that can be used to shield from public view who owns what. It is essential to remember that assessment records invariably are based on ownership of the property on a specific date — usually January 1 of each year.

Thus if a person acquires a property on May 20 of a given year, but sells it to another person or otherwise disposes of it before the following January 1, that person's ownership or interest in the property would **NOT** be reflected in the assessment or tax records.

Instead, the records would show the name of the party who was the listed owner on the January 1 preceding the May 20 acquisition date. Similarly, the record would show the name of the party our subject sold the property to before the end of the year.

For this reason, we must check both the grantor and grantee books for a given year in order to determine whether a person was involved in any transactions for that one-year period. Shortcuts are fine, but they can lead us astray at times.

Scattering the Straw Parties; Penetrating Smokescreens

IF YOU want to conceal your involvement in a real estate transaction, there are a lot of ways to do it.

Some public officials have been known to become expert at it. Private individuals and corporations do it all the time. Often it can be for a clearly legitimate reason — such as trying to acquire property at a reasonable price.

At other times, it may be to shield a political payoff, bribe or protect against disclosure of a conflict of interest that would be frowned on. The methods of concealing one's role can be as numerous as an accomplished con artist's repertoire of tricks.

A partial listing includes use of relatives, straw parties, dummy corporations, land trusts, out-of state companies, documents which are executed but never filed and the bouncing of properties from one party to others like a ricocheting handball.

But no matter how imaginative an approach is used, it is often possible for you to push aside the curtain of secrecy and discover a hidden involvement.

At other times, however, some masters of maneuvering create such a labyrinth of paper corporations and pseudo-document trails that it is impossible to prove a particular party had a hand in the deal. You might suspect their involvement, but still lack the link necessary to prove it.

Often what you must do is to put yourself in the place of the person or corporation you are investigating. If you were in their place, what would you do? What specific steps would you take? How could you cover your trail? Where might the records be that would show what you have done? Can you get at the records yourself? If not, do you know someone, or can you get to know someone, who could get at the records? What appeals could you make to that person to help you?

If your investigation leads you into an area that

you know little about, you should try to enlist the aid of an expert in that field.

If you are checking on banking practices, for example, it would be logical to go to a bank official or employee you trust and ask him or her to help you understand the processes involved. Similarly, if you were checking out an insurance company or transaction, you would do well to seek out the help and counsel of a disinterested insurance agent or broker.

The one thing you want to avoid is asking help from someone who might know and be friendly to the subject being investigated. You might be talking to a carrier of tales.

Knowing the step-by-step process involved in the kind of transaction you are interested in can often lead you to documents and records that you otherwise might never know existed.

In my own experience, the knowledge that banks routinely microfilm all checks and deposit tickets that they process each day once helped me prove that a public official had embezzled more than $25,000 in fire district funds and funneled them into his own automobile dealership bank account through an ingenious and, of course, illegal scheme.

We will go into more detail later about the importance of knowing how the bureaucratic process works.

Let's say you suspect that a city official in your community profitted from the sale of land or property to the city. You know, however, that the official's name did not appear in the news accounts or public announcements about the transaction.

In such a case, it is still possible that the official had a very direct interest in the city's purchase. If

"The knowledge that banks routinely microfilm all checks helped prove embezzlement of more than $25,000."

you examine the real estate records as I suggested, you would compile a history of all his or her property dealings. In doing so, you might discover that although another person was listed as owner of the land at issue when it was sold to the city, that person had actually obtained it from the city official.

By tracing the history of the parcel the city bought, you would show that at one point the official had owned it and then conveyed title to someone else, who in turn sold it to the city. Next you might be able to find out how much the city official had paid for it and how this compared to the price the city paid.

If the official took out a loan or mortgage on the property when he acquired it, you could easily find out the amount of the loan involved, in most instances. You might also be able to speculate somewhat accurately about the down payment, or possibly find out from other sources what the total price was.

These other sources might include the person who actually sold or transferred the property to the city official or possibly title company pesonnel who helped handle the technicalities of the transaction.

Checking of real estate records involving family members or close relatives of the official might provide a potentially excellent tip-off that would lead to disclosure of the official's ties with the transaction. If the official is a male and married, try to find out his spouse's maiden name and check records relating to her parents and family.

Sometimes, it pays to check the dealings of persons who have the same last name as the official, if you suspect a brother may have been used as a front man or straw party in the deal.

Or the official may have used an employee or a company in which he is an officer. He may have set up a company for the sole purpose of using it as a front to conceal his involvement.

If this was done, you could check records at the Secretary of State's office and attempt to learn the identity of the principals in the firm.

In most states, corporations doing business are required to submit annual reports listing their officers and directors. Often this material is submitted to the state by a person who is officially designated as the firm's registered agent. Or it may be forwarded to the state on stationery belonging to a particular attorney. Thus the employee or the accompanying letter that was sent to the state may give you a clue as to the persons who were involved in

the city property purchase, but whose names might not have appeared either in the land records or in the roster of company officers.

If, as suggested, you were to check all property records relating to the city official over a number of years, you might chance upon dealings linking his or her name to various corporate real estate transactions. A close examination of those deeds might disclose revealing addresses or show that he or she was listed as an officer of the firm.

Suppose when you checked the records relating to the official that you found he or she was involved in two companies with offices at 801 Clagore Avenue. Then suppose that the city bought the land in question from a different company with the same address.

This could be a coincidence, of course. But it might also be a tip-off that the official has links to this firm.

On the basis of documents filed with a county or

city, a straw party might appear to be the sole owner of a property. Or the records might indicate he or she had acquired title to it but later disposed of it. But in reality, the straw party had little, if any, interest in the transactions. Straw parties often are simply middlemen for record purposes. At other times, they may be used as fronts or for cover-up purposes.

THEIR use, as we noted, can be for totally legitimate reasons.

One reason might simply be the convenience of having a secretary or an employee serve as the recipient of quit-claim deeds from multiple owners. Thus all the owners would relinquish claim to the property, and the secretary or employee could then transfer title to an agreed-upon third party or to one or more of the multiple owners. This frequently happens in cases involving heirs and estate matters.

The use of straw parties as fronts also is legitimate in the vast majority of cases. Many institutions, for example, might use a straw to avoid having the owner raise his asking price for a property because he knows the institution interested in it is a wealthy one.

Straw parties come in many shapes and forms. It could be a relative, friend, a janitor, housemaid, an employee, a real estate firm, banking or financial institution or an obscure firm or corporation established simply for that purpose.

Sometimes the straw party approach works like this: a person or company puts up the money for the purchase but has the seller transfer the property to the straw party's name. This deed is then filed. For public inspection purposes, it would appear that the straw party is the actual title-holder. But almost simultaneous with the deeding of the property to the straw, the persons actually behind the purchase would require that the straw sign a deed conveying the property to them. This deed, however, is not filed.

It remains, instead, in the possession of the real buyers. The deed may never be filed, but instead remain locked in a safe deposit box. At any time, the real owners can file their deed and thus negate the straw party's deed. Often the straw party may be paid only a minimal amount for serving in this capacity.

Or the straw may do it as part of his or her job.

But always there is the unfiled deed. It is the true purchaser's protection against being stripped of the property by an unscrupulous straw.

We have made the point that frequently it is not only difficult but impossible to detect the identity of

a person or firm using a straw party.

There are, however, many instances when you can get this information. One way that we suggested earlier is to make a detailed study of property transactions involving the person or firm that you suspect is using the straw.

Another way is to do the same thing for the straw party. Here you would be attempting to determine whom the straw previously has represented. You might find that the straw consistently at some point has received or conveyed title to the same group of persons or firms time and again. This might be a good tip-off, particularly if city directories list the straw as being employed in an apparent low-paying job that would seem to rule out extensive property holdings.

In such instances, the apparent straw party might merit some further study. It might be good to approach the person directly and ask what role he or she had in the transaction.

A foot-weary saleswoman in a bargain basement store may be an unknown real estate genius. Maybe she has parlayed thrift and shrewd investments and dealings into a fortune. But maybe not. If she has a menial job and lives in a rundown apartment in a low-rent area, the odds would suggest that her role was that of a straw.

There are other means of learning who are the real principals in a deal. In some communities where problems with arson have been encountered, authorities there may require that a register of straw parties be maintained. Sometimes the register is on file at the city or county Recorder of Deeds office, or with the fire marshal's office.

Often the names of commonly used straw parties are known to persons active and knowledgeable in the real estate field. And they can sometimes help you find out the true identity of the property-holder.

There is another frequently helpful avenue. This is in the tax arena. Because counties and communities throughout the nation rely on tax revenues, they must maintain mailing addresses of property-holders. Thus, although the name of the straw party may be listed on deed and tax records, the secret property-holder frequently uses a mailing address that he can be sure of.

The secret, or real, owner may be hesitant to have

"The true owner may resort to listing his own address for tax-bill mailing purposes."

a tax bill mailed to a straw party.

Suppose the straw loses it or ignores the bill and fails to pass it along to him. If this happens, authorities might put the property up for public sale for non-payment of taxes. So the true owner may resort to the safeguard of listing his own address for tax bill mailing purposes, or the address of a corporation that he owns or controls.

Frequently, this address may be identical to corporations that can be shown to be headed or owned by the person or parties we suspect may be the true owner.

VI. Many Uses of Land Records

That Wasn't the Boy Scouts, Madam; That Was the Mafia

A KIND, elderly lady helped teach me two lessons early in my reporting career. One is that an unlikely source can provide a valuable tip. The other lesson was the importance of being able to trace land and real estate records. I remember our first meeting.

"Please do have tea," she said, placing a saucer and cup on the wrought iron lawn table next to us. We were sitting in the shade of a semi-circle of large elm trees in the yard of her home in a quiet suburb west of Providence, Rhode Island. She had phoned earlier to the suburban news bureau that I then headed for the Providence Journal-Bulletin.

Over the phone she told me that she and her neighbors were upset by the constant littering of the roadway fronting their homes by passing trash haulers.

"We are at our wit's end. Can't you do something for us?" she implored. Normally I might have politely shrugged her off.

But because it was one of those enchanting spring days and because she sounded like a very nice elderly woman not given to needless griping, I agreed to stop by her home and talk to her. I did so, expecting it would be little more than a pleasant way to spend an afternoon hour or so. Maybe, I thought, I might write a few paragraphs about her and the neighbors' complaint.

If nothing else, I figured my visit might be a small step toward assuring residents of that small community that a metropolitan paper was interested enough to listen to their concerns.

But as it turned out, that telephone call and springday visit generated a series of front-page stories that ran for weeks and disclosed indiscriminate dumping of hundreds of tons of trash and garbage at a city dump owned and operated by New England Mafia chieftain Raymond Patriarca. The Mafia, it later developed, was not content just to use its own

59

land for dumping. It also dumped extensively on Boy Scout-owned land. But, of course it never asked anyone's permission and never told anyone what it was doing. Nor did it pay for its dumping privileges.

As we sat and sipped tea, she told me that she and her neighbors were dismayed by the trash and debris in front of their homes.

How could that be, I asked. She lived in a small, largely rural and residential community with virtually no industry or commercial development that would attract heavy traffic. Smithfield's eastern edge bordered on North Providence, Patriarca's hometown where politics and corruption often seemed allied.

But even as we spoke, I could not help noticing a steady caravan of garbage trucks and trash haulers winding past her home. A number of the trucks belonged to a firm that had contracts with the city of Pawtucket and other Rhode Island communities for waste disposal.

Because of landfill problems, Pawtucket had required the firm to dump trash collected in Pawtucket outside that city. Unknown to Smithfield officials and residents, their community had been chosen for an honor it never sought or wanted.

I followed one of the trucks and saw it enter a fenced area through an open gate. Luckily, there was a nearby hill that I was sure would provide a good vantage point to observe what was going on. I drove there, hid my car and climbed the hill.

During the next hour I saw truck after truck pull into a sprawling dump site and unload garbage and trash. They came from all over Rhode Island. A few bore signs showing they were from neighboring Massachusetts. I hurried back to the newspaper's main office and told them what I had seen and what I suspected.

The next day I returned, with binoculars and a photographer equipped with an array of cameras and long-range lenses. We climbed the hillside and staked out the dump site. We stayed there the entire day and returned the following two days — making a visual and written record. In the three days, we saw more than 100 vehicles dumping at the site. The photographer took sequence pictures showing the traffic, the payment of money by many dumpers and the extent of the dumping.

This phase completed, I began checking land and other municipal records. They showed that the neighboring city of North Providence had its town dump in Smithfield in the area we had been observing. But a check of the records showed that the city of North Providence did not own the dump. The dump was on land owned by Patriarca, the Mafia boss, who had quietly signed an agreement with North Providence officials. Under it, he allowed their city to dump there for a nominal yearly amount. Outsiders were also allowed to dump, provided they paid.

Patriarca, however, owned only one acre in Smithfield, the records showed. I knew that the dump site covered far more than one acre. My best guess was 12 to 15 acres. If so, Patriarca was allowing dumping on Boy Scout-owned land adjacent to his one-acre parcel. That's what was happening.

After the stories and photographs were published,

Smithfield and North Providence officials halted the unauthorized dumping. Surveyors moved in. They found that, indeed, most of the dumping had occurred on the Boy Scout land and that Patriarca's site had long ago been entirely covered.

At times it is critical that you be able to trace land and real estate records yourself, without having to rely on help from clerks or other public officials or employes. Many reporters and investigators have taught themselves to be competent researchers in this area. There is nothing to prevent you from doing the same.

"It is critical that you be able to trace records yourself, without having to rely on clerks."

Just recently one student in a class I teach on investigative reporting told me he wished he had taken the course the previous year.

"I would have saved myself a lot of time, money and grief," he said. The student, a 30-year-old telephone company employe, explained all the problems he and his wife had encountered after putting in a formal bid several months earlier on a home they were interested in buying.

They plunked down $500 earnest money. Only later did they learn that the lot was 10 feet less in width than they had thought. Worse yet, they discovered that 23 feet of their driveway ran over the property of the seller's sister. This came out when they had a title search made at a cost of about $400.

As this is written, the problems had not yet been resolved between the buyer and seller. Would the student and his wife have to pay for the added 10 feet and right-of-way for their driveway? Suppose the whole deal fell through. Would they be able to recover their $500 earnest money? What would it cost them to hire a lawyer to protect their interests? If they backed out of the deal could they ever recoup what they spent on the title search?

Even if everything was eventually worked out between the buyer and seller, the delays already encountered might see the mortgage rate they had to pay go higher.

If the student and his wife had been able to make a quick record check before putting in their bid on the home, they might well have gotten a hint of the troubles ahead. They would have been able to foresee the driveway problem and insisted it be ironed out before they put down their earnest money.

Or they could have asked themselves why go to the expense of having a title search on a problem-plagued property, when there were other desirable homes available and free of hitches. A little research could have spared them a lot of aggravation.

Records Showed Why Airport Property Was Flying So High

CHECKING land records often can be a tedious chore. But it can have its rewards.

Such was the case in 1972 when a tipster told me he had heard that a real estate broker who was a friend, political ally and one-time business associate of the then-St. Louis mayor had made a handsome commission on the sale of land to the city for airport expansion.

The tipster could offer little else in the way of help or guidance. He did not know the amount of the fee or what property was involved. He couldn't say when the transaction had occurred, but suspected it had been within about two years.

The broker's friendship and past business ties with the mayor were well known. So too was his undisputed clout with City Hall. But there never had been any public mention or indication of his having negotiated with the city on airport land.

The broker, a former Democratic ward committeeman in St. Louis, and the mayor once had been partners in a jitney taxicab firm. The firm was sold for $625,000 after the mayor had taken office to a public bus system serving the St. Louis area and a number of Illinois communities.

Given the tenuous nature of the tip about the real estate man's involvement in an airport land transaction, it seemed that checking it out would be like trying to isolate an unknown virus.

Yet within five weeks, we were able to report that the broker had been paid an $83,000 commission by the owner of a one-half acre improved tract which the city bought in 1969 to enlarge St. Louis Lambert Field.

The mayor's friend had represented the seller, who confirmed he initially had been offered between $150,000 and $160,000 by the city for the property.

With the broker's help, the seller got $260,000 for it. The final purchase price was an increase of about 60 per cent over what the owner had been offered by

65

the city before he retained the politically influential broker to handle the transaction.

The original tip, together with extensive and hard digging into the records, led to a broader inquiry that generated a long series of stories in the St. Louis Post-Dispatch detailing fee payments totaling more than $420,000 to politically prominent Democrats involved in airport land deals.

The beneficiaries included two state representatives who, as lawyers, negotiated with the city on behalf of private sellers.

Besides cozy political ties, the stories depicted a profitable playground of airport land transactions. They revealed lax purchasing and appraisal practices, inadequate or non-existent records, ignoring or suppression of appraisal reports and payments for work not performed.

"The original tip, together with extensive and hard digging, generated a long series of stories."

The initial series of articles appeared over a period of several weeks. But as often happens, they led to new trails and new revelations within a few months. In several instances, follow-up disclosures were published by the Post-Dispatch three or more years after the original series.

Articles ultimately sparked by the original vague tip alleging political cronyism in city airport dealings included disclosures that:

♦ Besides his $83,000 fee cited here earlier, the same broker and his real estate firm also got a $200,000 commission on a 1972 airport expansion acquisition. The fee was paid by owners of a private cemetery who sold the city an 8.74-acre tract there and an aerial flight easement over an adjacent cemetery parcel of about 12 acres.

The city paid $1,200,000 for the property and aerial easement. This was at least $600,000 more than it was worth on the basis of an appraisal made at the insistence of the Federal Aviation Administration. The FAA ordered the new appraisal after the Post-Dispatch had disclosed a great disparity between two earlier appraisals, one of which had been ignored and suppressed.

♦ Another real estate broker friendly to the same mayor was paid $18,275 for airport land appraisals he had not been involved in.

♦ Former state representative Richard J. Rabbitt, a St. Louis Democrat who later became speaker of the Missouri House of Representatives, received a legal fee of more than $100,000 in 1970 from a private property owner for negotiating the sale to the city of part of an amusement park for airport expansion. But more than five years after purchasing the property, the city still had not used it for airport purposes and had begun looking around for a possible buyer.

♦ Another attorney and prominent St. Louis Democrat also got a fee for representing a private owner involved in airport property negotiations. The size of the fee was never disclosed. At the time of the transaction, the attorney was a state representative. He subsequently became a city official and later was appointed a state judge.

When I first got the tip nearly a decade ago that touched off my interest in airport land dealings, I had little to go on. The only thing the tipster could tell me was that he had heard that the broker who was a friend of the mayor had gotten a fee on some airport transactions.

But which one and when? How to prove it? Was it even true? Given the scant nature of the tip, I felt I had no choice but to examine the records relating to all airport land dealings over an extended period dating back perhaps 10 years.

That is exactly what I attempted to do. Step by step, I reconstructed from real estate records the entire airport, using the techniques mentioned here earlier. Plat maps depicting the airport complex were examined. I reviewed each parcel and recorded a brief history of all parcels that had been acquired by the airport in the previous 10 years.

"Step by step, I reconstructed the entire airport from real estate records."

Doubtless it would have saved me a little time to go back into the records only five years, but I felt that the longer period would give me a better perspective of how the airport had been expanded.

In the case of parcels acquired during the preceding decade, I recorded the names of the persons or parties who sold properties to the city, the date of the transactions, the purchase prices as reflected on the deeds and the names of anyone who signed or witnessed the documents on behalf of any party.

I also made a note of any addresses, notaries public and references to any ordinances or legislation authorizing the city's purchases, as well as the source of funding.

Although Lambert Field is owned by the city of St. Louis, it is located in St. Louis County. That meant that the land records I wanted to check were on file in the county recorder of deeds office. But there also was a maze of records to check at St. Louis City Hall, including airport budget accounts and minutes of meetings of two city boards which had to approve the purchase. One was the city's three-member Board of Estimate and Apportionment. The other was the city's airport commission.

Nowhere did the broker's name appear in the records I examined. By reviewing all the data I had collected and focusing on 25 specific transactions within the preceding three years, I was able to narrow the list of property owners that the broker may have represented in airport land sales to a few names.

Finally, I settled on the half-acre parcel that I felt best fit the few sketchy details given me by the tipster.

In the meantime, I learned from other sources that the broker's fee had been in the $80,000 range.

But at that point, I still was not sure which land deal was involved. I felt fairly certain, however, that the seller probably was a St. Louis businessman who was president of a petroleum company that owned about 125 gasoline stations. But could I prove he had paid a comission to the broker? And who better to confirm it than the businessman himself?

The next logical step seemed clear. I could not approach the businessman empty-handed and expect him to confide in me. The odds were too long. But if I could convince him that I knew all about the transaction, this might give me the leverage I needed.

With this in mind, I began to delve into the businessman's background and learn everything I possibly could about him. For more than a week, I dug for every record and scrap of information that might help. Before I was done, I had a hefty file on him. It included information about his business dealings, family, zoning applications, driving record, credit rating and financial stature.

"I began to delve into the man's background and learn everything I could about him."

I checked every newspaper clipping I could find, not only in the city's two major dailies but also the suburban weeklies. One clipping mentioned a prize the businessman's daughter had won in horseback riding.

Accompanied by William Freivogel, another Post-Dispatch reporter, I dropped by his office unannounced and asked to speak to him. We chatted about the oil industry in general and then about his own business. As we spoke, I spread out on the desk before us part of the thick file we had compiled relating to him and the airport land sale.

"The businessman leaned back in his chair, seemingly stunned by what we knew."

When he began to tell how many service stations his firm operated, we supplied the number before he could say it. There was a photograph on the wall in front of his desk. It showed his daughter and a horseback-riding award she had won. As he was about to tell us about her prize, we identified it.

The businessman leaned back in his chair, seemingly stunned by what we knew.

"Now," I said, "Let's discuss the airport deal."

We then reviewed the transaction, step by step. At first, he provided only one word answers. But as the extent of our knowledge became clear, he began opening up. Right at the outset, we referred to the broker by name and asked him if he felt the broker had done a good job negotiating with the city for him.

"Yeah," he responded.

Bingo. The question had been asked in an off-hand manner, but the answer was critical to us.

As the interview progressed, he said the city had first offered him $150,000 to $160,000 for the property. Believing this was too low, he said he retained the broker to try to get a better price. He added that the broker had handled various real estate transactions for him and his firm over a period of about 20 years.

Under their arrangement on the airport transaction, he said, the broker was to receive any amount he could negotiate with the city in excess of $175,000. This was a vital piece of information for us. We knew that after an allowance for taxes, the city had paid $258,161 for the property. We did some quick mental math.

"That means you paid him a commission of about $83,000," we said.

"Yeah, that's right," the seller replied.

Bingo, again. The rest of the interview was a cake walk.

Later we spoke by phone to the broker involved. He also confirmed his role in the transaction. He said he had never sought and was never accorded favored treatment by city officials based on his long-time friendship and political association with the mayor.

"It was a very fine commission," the broker said. "I devoted a lot of time and effort to the negotiations . . . I think the city got a fair and good deal."

The mayor said he hadn't known his friend had any role in the negotiations.

At the time, I did not realize that later I would again be asking the same broker pretty much the same questions about another airport land transaction.

During the course of my airport study, I spoke to a number of owners who had sold property in the previous few years for expansion of Lambert Field. One owner said a "mutual business acquaintance" had arranged a meeting between himself and a state representative who appeared interested in helping with some phase of the negotiations.

"He (the state representative) said maybe we should go down there, City Hall, I imagine and help a little," the owner recounted. "I said, 'I don't need you.' He wanted I guess to make a little extra money, but he wasn't going to make it off me."

After the story about the broker's $83,000 fee appeared, a City Hall friend suggested that I take a closer look at the airport land purchase involving part of Washington Park Cemetery. For decades the cemetery had been used extensively for burial by black families in the St. Louis area.

The city paid $1,009,000 for a nearly nine-acre tract at the cemetery and $191,000 for a flight easement over an adjacent 12-acre parcel there. This latter payment was what my friend found particularly

"Calculations indicated that the city ultimately paid perhaps $350,000 more than it should have."

puzzling.

"Why on earth would the city pay that much to fly over part of a cemetery where there are damn few monuments higher than six feet?" he asked.

Partly at his urging, I again checked the records on the purchase. On the surface, there seemed nothing out of the ordinary other than the novelty of the aerial easement payment. The prices paid by the city for both the nine-acre parcel and the flight easement were virtually identical to valuations recommended by a real estate appraiser hired by the city.

One question readily came to mind, however. Why did the city rely totally on a single appraisal, especially in a $1.2-million transaction? That bothered me. It also prompted me to again review every expenditure from airport funds during the year at issue.

The review was an eye-opener. As I glanced through page after page of monthly computer print-outs, I came across the bill and payment for the cemetery appraisal. That was no surprise. But then as I examined ledgers showing airport expenditures earlier that year, I stumbled across an interesting entry.

It showed that another appraisal had been submitted and paid for three months before the appraisal that had been made part of the transaction record. But this earlier appraisal, despite having been made by a firm considered by some in the field as a leading authority on cemetery appraisals, had been ignored and suppressed.

Although it did not encompass the flight easement, its calculations indicated that the city ultimately paid perhaps $350,000 more than it should have for the nearly nine acres that it purchased outright.

That earlier appraisal was nowhere to be found in the city files — as least in those files open to public inspection.

To obtain a copy of the report, I had to contact the

firm that had made the appraisal. While talking to an officer of the firm, he mentioned in an off-hand manner that shortly after the sale of the cemetery property he had bumped into one of the co-owners.

"I told him they were lucky to get such a high price for it and that I thought the city had paid more than the property was worth," the appraiser recalled. It was at this point, he said, that the seller agreed the price had been a good one, but added that he and his partner actually had received less than $1,000,000 of the $1,200,000 purchase price.

"Frankly, I was taken aback when he told me that," the appraiser said.

"But I didn't pursue the subject. I thought I might be about to hear something that perhaps I would be better off not knowing." He said he was still puzzled by what the man meant.

A few days later, I wrote a story about the transaction, including the wide disparity in the appraisal valuations. The co-owners would not disclose any details of the negotiations. Nor would they say who had represented them. Once the story was published, I began to research the land deal more extensively and the background of the principals involved.

Meanwhile, the Federal Aviation Administration, on the basis of my initial article, ordered a new appraisal, which concluded that the city had paid

more than twice what it should have for the nine-acre tract and the adjacent aerial easement.

On the basis of its appraisal, the FAA sharply reduced the amount of federal funds it would reimburse the city for that phase of the Lambert Field expansion.

But aside from these developments, I had uncovered little else about the transaction that appeared newsworthy. My research, for example, did not reveal who had negotiated with the city on behalf of the sellers. Although I had my suspicions, I could not then prove who had filled this role.

Nor did my efforts turn up anything that would shed light on the remark by one of the co-owners that they had received several hundred thousand dollars less than the $1.2-million recorded sales price.

Records relating to the transaction showed they had received the full amount. So what could he have been alluding to?

My research had uncovered a lot of data about the sellers, their property holdings and dealings, as well as other related matters. But the inquiry was at a dead-end. Given this, I had no choice but to put the project aside and hope for a break.

Several years later, there was an unexpected and unforeseen break. In the summer of 1975, I learned that the principal owner of the cemetery and his wife were in the midst of a long contested divorce action.

The file in the case was voluminous. Inspecting the exhibits and depositions on file, I came across an income tax report. It contained a reference to a $200,000 consultant fee paid with a cashier's check in connection with the land and flight easement sale.

The tax return, however, did not identify whom the money was paid to. Both parties in the divorce and their attorneys refused to disclose the recipient.

Fortunately, the husband's deposition in the case dealt at some length with the airport transaction. It also revealed that a $200,000 fee had been paid to a consultant who handled some of the negotiations. But again, the payee was not identified. It did, however, give the date of the cashier's check and the bank it had been drawn on.

These two bits of information proved invaluable. They were the clues that helped me identify the recipient of the $200,000. It was the same broker who had received an $83,000 fee on the earlier airport transaction.

In order to uncover this, I first learned everything I could about how cashier's checks are handled and what banking and other records relating to them are kept. Then it was a question of who might have access to this information, and what I could do to confirm it or have someone confirm it for me? This phase alone took several weeks.

Rarely Does a Single Morsel Stretch Into a Free Lunch

MANY of us with an investigative frame of mind may be tempted at times to fantasize. In the dream, a tipster bent on exposing corruption or wrongdoing, single-handedly provides a detailed rundown on a scandal that ought to be made public. The tipster not only lays out how the scandal works and who is involved, but also has documents and proof of his charges.

Unfortunately, it is a fantasy that rarely reflects reality. Most volunteer tips are worthless. Experienced investigators have learned that most tipsters prove unreliable and have little information of value.

Too often, tipsters do not know, understand or interpret correctly what they have seen or heard. They may be incapable of distinguishing between facts and gossip.

Their motives may be admirable — a sense of righteous indignation at some affront to commonly shared ideals. Sometimes the motive is as rampant and trivial as the human compulsion to gossip. But often the tipster is motivated not by idealism, but simply by revenge.

In dealing with tipsters, it pays to be patient and a good listener. Although they may be wrong or off base an overwhelming percentage of the time, there is always the possibility they may be right this time around. Just because what they say seems unlikely or even preposterous, this does not mean they are wrong.

Their motive in telling you something, whether it be prompted by idealism or revenge, should not be a deciding factor. What counts is whether the information is factual or can be shown to be accurate.

Even a convicted felon or person with a reputation as a shameless gossip can be telling the truth. You have to ask yourself if it is worth your time and effort to check out what he or she is saying.

If a tipster has built a reputation of being generally reliable, it may make your decision on whether to investigate much easier.

But just as disease and illness pay no heed to social stature, class or wealth, the value of a tip often bears no relationship to a person's title or employment. A discredited politician or a jail inmate may provide the key to a major expose. Or it could come from a clerical employee, a janitor, nursing home resident, or the untutored, inarticulate laborer.

Police investigators, law enforcement agencies, detectives and investigative journalists often make it a point to try to cultivate a wide variety of sources of information, including tipsters. They like tipsters with good track records. Similarly, the tipster who sees his tip materialize into something is more likely to return with a new tidbit to be checked on.

Jack Anderson, the Pulitzer Prize winning syndicated columnist, constantly is flooded with tips and classified documents that result in stunning revelations about governmental or military waste and irregularities. Anderson's success is no accident. He has worked for years at cultivating sources who know they can trust him to protect their identity.

Few of us are as persistent or persuasive as Anderson. But whether we are experienced investigators or lay persons with little or no training in the field, we can try to impart to those whom we are seeking information from, our sincerity and indignation over what has happened.

Many people might like to help. Often, however, they hesitate to tell what they know for fear of losing their jobs or other reprisals. They must be able to count on your not disclosing their role. If you betray such a pledge to a source, chances are that word of this will leak out. When that happens, why would anyone want to take you at your word again?

The need to nurture and respect such trust goes beyond legalistic arguments, in my view.

Reporters cite First Amendment rights in arguing against being compelled to disclose confidential sources. And properly so, in most cases. A number of states have recognized the right of reporters to protect the identity of their sources and have enacted so-called shield laws.

But constitutional issues aside, I believe there is a more personal but fundamental point at stake. It is the keeping of one's word. A promise not to reveal the identity of a source is just that — a promise.

It is an act of faith between two persons. Violate it and you surrender an important part of yourself.

Even when a tipster is on target with his information or has a record of reliability, what he has to say generally is just a starting point or entering wedge.

You must take it from there and hope that hard work, imaginative digging and a little luck will pay off. You can not count on a corrupt politician, public official or business man being careless and stupid enough to leave evidence of his guilt littering the landscape.

Bob Woodward and Carl Bernstein, the two Washington Post reporters who helped break open the Watergate scandal and force the resignation of President Richard M. Nixon, made good use of numerous sources they cultivated while investigating the break-in at the Democratic national headquarters in Washington and the Nixon Administration's subsequent cover-up efforts. Perhaps no single source has been the subject of more publicity and speculation than Woodward's source, an executive branch official identified only as "Deep Throat."

These sources were invaluable to the two reporters.

But the real key to their success was their relentless pursuit of a scandal that most Americans did not perceive, including most of the news media. They felt driven to follow every lead and to make unannounced night visits to the homes of employees and officials of Nixon's mammoth fund-raising

committee. Doors repeatedly were slammed in their faces. Eventually, however, a few employees and one former committee official were willing to talk to them.

Tipsters and sources can make an investigator's work a lot easier.

But often a tip does not come from an outsider. It frequently originates in the mind of the investigator. Something about a situation may strike you as unusual. That could be your mind relaying a tip that merits checking. Or there seems to be a pattern of events that may be more than a coincidence.

Sometimes, for example, a routine check of expenditures by a governmental or corporate entity will turn up payments that add up to tens of thousands of dollars to one company for vague or questionable services. This could be, in effect, a self-generated tip that might lead to disclosures of improprieties that were not even envisioned prior to the fiscal review.

IX. Understanding Public Finances

Your Checkbook Can Explain Complex Government Budgets

SOME of us have trouble balancing our personal budget. So it is not too surprising that we might be awed by the prospect of trying to comprehend our city or state budget.

How does one cope with budgets involving expenditures that run into hundreds of thousands or millions of dollars?

The answer is as simple as your checkbook.

You know what information you list in your checkbook. Your checking account has a specific number. The checkbook lists the number of each check, the date the check was issued, the recipient and the amount of the check.

Often we also include a brief explanation of what the money was being spent on. There are also two other important entries: the beginning balance and the running balance.

Another thing worth remembering is that ultimately the check returns to our possession. But before it gets back to us, it is microfilmed by the bank cashing it, as well as by your own bank. The banks also microfilm all deposit and withdrawal slips, usually on a daily basis.

As individuals, most of us keep one checking account. In a family, there may be several checking accounts.

In contrast, a small community might have scores of checking accounts. The number of accounts in a big city budget might run into the hundreds or thousands. So, too, with state government. The awesome federal budget, as mammoth as it is, should be viewed as a series of separate checking accounts.

On a federal level, the accounts would number in the hundreds of thousands. The principle, however, is still the same.

Let's pretend you want to check out the budget and expenditures of a small community.

Regardless of the size of the town or city you are

dealing with, you should be able to see how every cent is spent, just as you would with your own checking account. A city police department, for example, may have a budget of $200,000. In all likelihood, the departmental budget probably would be broken down into a number of categories.

The major category might cover salaries. Another would be devoted to equipment purchases and still another to equipment repairs. Separate accounts might be maintained for uniforms, health and welfare benefits, radio and communications, and funds for informants or undercover drug purchases.

At the start of a municipality's fiscal year, each department normally is credited with a specific budgetary allocation. As each dollar is spent, the department's operating balance reflects a corresponding reduction.

In some cases, the balance is increased by incoming revenues during the fiscal year. But usually these go the general treasury or specific accounts, sometimes to the department where the fees originated.

But by going down the department's ledger, just as you would review your checkbook entries line by line, you can trace each penny spent. If you cannot, then the records are inadequate or incomplete, perhaps deliberately so.

Depending on the community's size, the ledgers may be handwritten or in the form of periodic computer print-outs. But they must list each expenditure, to whom it was made, the date and amount.

The ledgers should also list a voucher number.

This is a key item. It usually can lead you not only to the requisition form, if any, that was submitted in support of a requested purchase or expenditure, but also the supplier's billing or receipt.

The voucher should identify what services or goods the money was spent on.

"You should be able to see how every cent is spent, just as you would with your own checking account."

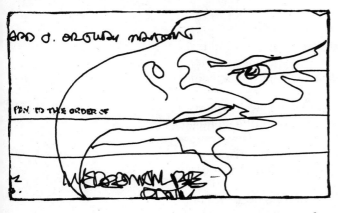

An examination of vouchers often can be revealing. Inspecting records of one Illinois school system, for example, a reporter found that the district had purchased tens of thousands of light bulbs. It had enough of them stored away to last a much larger school system for nearly a decade.

Over the years, I have tried to make it a practice to routinely check spending records of individual agencies or programs. That is a good way to begin attacking a budget. Rather than attempting to evaluate a municipality's overall budget, it often is better to take a detailed look at just one phase of the budget.

Without devoting weeks or months to the task, it is difficult for even an expert to draw valid broad conclusions about how wisely and effictively a town or city spends its money.

But it often is possible to do this for a single department or government activity. The findings of such a limited but in-depth examination may well prove unassailable and be indicative of more widespread fiscal and budget management shortcomings.

One approach that frequently pays dividends is to focus on those areas that may have aroused your concern or suspicions. You may be incensed at the way the city maintains its streets or handles snow removal.

Or maybe you feel it is wasting money on consultants whose reports invariably are left to gather dust. Perhaps, you think your city is funneling contracts to political favorites or even to firms with ties to city officials.

If you want to, you can make a good stab at checking such things out. A close-up look at specific budget accounts involved may help you find the records needed to prove what is happening.

Let's say you are interested in highway spending and contracts.

In such a case, you would do well to start examining the highway department's budget, beginning with the ledger that shows those expenditures from the very start of the fiscal year. Take note of the budget allocation or starting balance.

Then go through every major highway account week by week and month by month. Don't try to absorb all the information the first time around. Instead, just race through the ledger pages showing the amounts paid out and the names of the recipients. You are not looking for details at this point, but merely trying to gain impressions.

As you move through records covering several months or more, or even two or three years, do names of certain recipients appear time and again? Does there seem to be a pattern of domination by one or several suppliers?

On this first glimpse through, pay particular attention to large expenditures. Do they seem concentrated among a few individuals or firms? Do expense account items seem excessive? Are there any expenditures listed that seem peculiar, like massive spending for asphalt and road-building materials in a community that long has neglected its streets?

As you gather impressions make a note of those things that pique your interest. Then start all over again and this time list all payments that might bear a more detailed look. Jot down the amounts, the dates paid, the voucher numbers and the budget accounts that the money was taken from.

Then have the vouchers pulled and examine them closely. Make notes on what the money was supposedly spent on, as well as the addresses of the firms or persons who received the payments. Be sure to list the quantities and unit prices of the purchases. Also make note of any reference as to who approved the purchase and under what ordinance, contract or other authority, if this information is included.

You might want to ask for photostats of some of

the records.

Once you have catalogued total spending for certain supplies or services, you can then begin taking a close look at who the suppliers are. The Yellow Pages in your local telephone directories would be a sensible starting point. Or you may want to look at a Polk directory, if there is one for your community.

You could contact your secretary of state's office for any incorporation records and annual reports of officers filed by the firms you may be interested in. You might want to review real estate records to see if the principals have had private property transactions with officials of your community.

"Once you have catalogued spending, you can then take a close look at who the suppliers are."

Were purchases made under contracts awarded by the city? The contracts may have been won under formal, competitive bidding. But maybe they were handed out without other firms getting a chance to bid. If there was formal bidding, the city should be able to produce records documenting this. Examine the contracts, the list of bidders and the bid specifications. You may want to insist that you be shown the bidding notice and the voucher that reflects payment to a newspaper that carried the legal advertisement.

Do other records show that the city's governing body or an official with authority to do so had approved the seeking and awarding of contracts?

You might want to check to see if the owners and officers of firms that benefitted from city business also contributed to political campaigns of public officials involved.

But even when a municipality or state government resorts to formal bidding, this does not necessarily mean that everything is on the up and up. There have been repeated instances where some companies submitted bids that would have provided little, if any, profit, but with the knowledge that once they got the contract they could count on later getting approval of profitable project revisions or change-orders.

A change-order often is necessary because plans for a project have to be revised for reasons that could not be foreseen. There may be unexpected drainage or construction problems, for example.

Most such revisions undoubtedly are valid. But not always are cost over-runs justified.

The change orders may simply be a handy device for assuring a low bidder that he later can pick up a handsome piece of additional change without the bother of the bidding process. This is because the price tags on change-orders usually are negotiated between the sponsoring agency and the contractor involved.

Be alert to patterns that may tip off what is happening. This may be the case where seemingly favored contractors narrowly win one bidding war after another on projects later marked by numerous revisions and costly change orders.

Often it is virtually impossible for a lay person to determine if the added costs were justified, especially when the purported extra work may be concealed behind walls and beneath ceilings.

But it may be possible at times to establish that the costs seem exorbitant. Or perhaps it can be shown that the add-on features had been considered and rejected when the original bid specifications were being drawn up. A pattern of repeated cost over-runs might be indicative of faulty planning, possibly with intent.

You might want to compare your city's expenditures for supplies or services with those in other communities. For example, is your town's per-mile road resurfacing costs way out of line with what neighboring towns of similar size and resources are paying?

Just because everything about a contract may seem totally proper on the surface, this does not necessarily make it so. Appearances can be deceiving.

Perhaps a contract called for resurfacing a total of 1.3 miles of streets with a four-inch overlay of asphalt. And maybe only two or three inches of asphalt were put down. And maybe the actual work covered slightly less than a mile. These are things that can be physically checked.

My own experience has taught me time and again the value of checking on contract compliance.

One such instance came after I had written a story disclosing that a St. Louis supply commissioner had gone on pleasure and vacation trips to Las Vegas, London, Hawaii and a resort in Alabama with an officer of a firm whose competitor the commissioner had sought to disqualify from obtaining a city street equipment contract.

If he had succeeded, the contract would have gone to his friend, a heavy equipment dealer. The official acknowledged that the two men and their wives had gone on the trips together, but denied he tried to favor his friend by intervening on his behalf in the contract award.

A few days after the story appeared, a tipster urged that I look into a rental contract the supply commissioner's friend had been awarded to provide warning-light barriers for city street work.

Nothing about the contract award seemed wrong.

Bids had been formally advertised and the supply commissioner's friend won on the basis of submitting the second-lowest bid. The low bidder was disqualified because the barriers he proposed to lease to the city did not comply with the specs. The supply commissioner's friend beat out the third-lowest bidder by about five cents a unit. So everything seemed proper.

But remember the six-sided transparent photo cube we cited earlier as a mental investigative aid. If the contract award was unflawed, I asked myself, could there have been some other irregularity?

One possible answer was that perhaps the friend's barriers also did not comply with the bid specifications. This turned out to be the case.

A tour of city streets to inspect barriers supplied by the friend's firm was revealing. It disclosed that cheaper units had been provided in each instance and that no one had enforced the bid specs. The barriers and warning lights differed markedly from what the city had contracted for.

Not too long after the incident, the supply commissioner resigned.

Attention to budgetary details can be rewarding.

While reviewing telephone vouchers, Post-Dispatch reporter William C. Lhotka discovered that an influential Missouri state senator had been burning up the long distance lines with more than $2,000 worth of calls to a woman friend and billing it to his state credit card.

Lhotka decided to look at the phone billings after the senator had interceded in the woman's behalf in a dispute involving a state agency.

"If the contract award was unflawed, I asked myself, could there be some other irregularity?"

In some states and communities, the task of checking out how much business they do with a particular company or vendor may be relatively easy. This is true where the municipality or state maintains a computerized listing of all vendors and payments to them over a given period.

Up to this point, we have focused on tracking expenditures of public funds. But spending data are only part of the budgetary picture. Equally important are government revenues. Budgets usually list major categories of income. Because various receipts and other revenues often become intermingled, it frequently is extremely difficult to pinpoint the source of each dollar received. It can be done at times, however, at least on a departmental or agency level.

"Review budget data back several years or more . . . it may show a pattern of large annual surpluses."

In examining state or municipal finances, it invariably is a good idea to see how governments invest tax revenues and other funds during the time the money is not immediately needed.

Is your state or community keeping large amounts of money in non-interest-bearing bank accounts? If interest is being earned, how does the rate compare to rates paid by other banks or other investments, such as Treasury Bills and certificates of deposit?

Are some banks getting favored treatment? Do city or state officials have ties to these banks? Perhaps as directors or officers? Are the bankers contributing heavily to campaign and election races? Are other banks being allowed to compete for fund deposits through the bidding process? Have favored banks made real estate loans to those officials who select the banking depositories?

You may want to review budget data dating back several years or more. This would help give you an idea whether spending and revenue projections have consistently been way off target. Or perhaps it may show a pattern of needlessly large annual surpluses.

Such an overview based on inspection of fiscal records for a number of years might reveal hidden deficits or other gimmicks used to conceal a community's true financial status. Your community may put off paying a lot of bills until the start of a new fiscal year, or it may be borrowing excessively to keep afloat.

Some budgetary areas that may be worth looking at include:

♦ Insurance coverage: Has a single agent or insurance firm been allowed to write all of a municipality's coverage for many years, with other firms being excluded from the business? Who decides on what coverage will be purchased, and do the decision-makers share in the premium commissions?

♦ Expense accounts, travel and conventions: Do expenditures in these categories seem reasonable or excessive? Are officials on expense accounts required to document what the money was spent on? When they attend conventions, do the events seem to relate to their public duties?

♦ Fiscal record-keeping: Are the records well maintained, with all expenditures documented? Can you trace every dollar spent out of a budgeted account? When was the last time there was a formal audit by the state or an independent auditing firm? Was the scope and purpose of the audit adequate to uncover potential fiscal problem areas?

♦ Supplies and other purchases: Is your community paying more for the same products or services than other roughly equivalent towns? Is there a centralized buying system, with formal bidding required on purchases over a certain amount?

Bureaucracy of Government Marches On, Step by Step

W E tend to be creatures of habit. As adults, we often become set in our ways, taking comfort in doing things in a rote-like manner that rarely varies. So too with governmental bureaucracies and many private companies and entrepreneurs.

This applies particularly to government agencies that must comply with public demands for accountability in their transactions and dealings.

Thus in budget matters, for example, the records kept by a small community may differ little in essential details from those maintained by a much larger city or state government. The same is true of taxes, assessments, supply purchases, municipal services and utility billings.

There are a number of reasons for uniformity of record-keeping procedures. Often it is dictated by sound business practices. Or the need for economy or efficiency.

For this reason, it is important that an investigator thoroughly know the process being used. It is good to have an overview or general understanding. But that may not be enough. Often you may need to know the process in tedious detail.

Any step in the paper trail, no matter how irrelevant it may seem, could be the crucial one. You might miss a piece of vitally needed information simply by being unaware of all procedural steps followed by a governmental bureaucracy or private enterprise.

Blessed are the bureaucracies, we said earlier in this book. They may generate needless red tape and cause frustrating delays. By their nature, however, they spawn a paper trail littered with carbon or photostatic copies.

Let us assume for a moment that you are interested in checking on how your town or city assesses and collects taxes.

One way to get to know the process is to check every detail about how your own tax bill was arrived

93

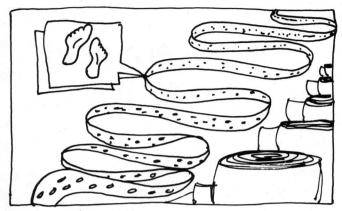

at. Go to the assessor's office and ask for a step-by-step explanation. Take mental notes, or better still written notes.

There are a lot of questions you might ask. When was your tax first set at its present level? Which employe or official made the assessment or valuation on which the tax was based? What records or notes were kept by the assessor's staff?

How many copies of the records exist? Who has the copies? Which specific persons or employes? How long must the records be kept on file? Where are they kept? If they date back many years, are they on microfilm or stored away in dust-covered boxes? Ask to see them.

Since the assessor's office in most communities does not actually collect the taxes, the assessor in these instances is required to provide the collector's office with a listing of taxpayers and their assessments. Thus — at least in this instance — the collector has a duplicate of records prepared by the assessor.

Should you want to, you could trace the valuations on a property over a period of years and determine whether the taxes have been paid or are still outstanding.

If you want to investigate a city or county assessor's office for possible favored treatment for certain officials or taxpayers, you could check the collector's records. With a little discretion and luck, you might be able to carry it off without tipping your hand or arousing suspicions about what you are up to.

Conversely, you might be able to get a good lead from the assessor's records on what kind of a job the collector is doing. Have taxes owed by officials, friends or favored property owners been allowed to remain delinquent for excessive periods?

Once you know the process involved, whether it relates to levying taxes or purchasing equipment or supplies, you can check virtually every detail of a transaction and analyze it.

"Once you know the process involved, you can check virtually every detail of an transaction and analyze it."

A Corporation Is Just a Body, But It Behaves Like a Person

THERE are many reasons you may want to investigate a particular business. And there are many different ways to go about it.

One good way to get started is to think of the business as a person. Human activities generate a trail of clues and records, many of which you can lawfully inspect. So too with corporate entities.

Just as Shakespeare gave us insight into the seven stages of man, we can find stages of corporate growth. Think of things we do as individuals and simply apply these activities to corporations or partnerships.

Man's first recorded event is birth, of course. We document it with a birth certificate. Similarly, when most businesses come into being, their arrival is duly recorded in the public archives. Often it is in the form of articles of incorporation that are filed with the Secretary of State's office.

Depending on the state you live in, the names of the actual incorporators may be on public record. Or the state may require that only one name be listed, usually that of the attorney who handled the filing.

The incorporation papers also set forth the general purpose of the new company, as well as the number of shares of stock it commences business with and the total number of shares it is authorized to issue. In all likelihood, the documents identify and list the address of the person or firm designated as the new corporation's registered agent. If a firm changes its name or revises its charter, these actions will be documented in the state files.

As individuals, we mark the passage of each year with a birthday observance. So, too, with corporations that report their status to stockholders each year. In many states, corporations are required to file annual reports with the Secretary of State.

These reports list the names of officers and directors of the firm, as well as its registered agent. By examining such annual reports over a period of

97

years, we can take note of any changes in the listing of those persons who head the company. This might provide valuable clues to shifts in ownership and control.

By law, the vast majority of firms are not required to make public their list of stockholders. Thus, once a company is formed, control of the firm could be lodged or transferred to a party operating behind the scenes and whose identity might never appear on the public record.

In the same way that a school report card reflects educational progress, a firm's annual financial report to its shareholders is a guage of how well it fared in the preceding fiscal year.

And corporations, like people, grow into adulthood and generate a trail of records along the way.

Next, we may marry — an event that is noted in the public records even if we send no notices or invitations to friends. So, too, with corporate mergers. They find their way into state records and the knowledge of many in the financial community.

Let's look at some other activities common to individuals and corporations.

Both often acquire and dispose of property and become obligated to pay property taxes. All of this we can search out in real estate records. We can compile a history of all property transactions and holdings by a firm and its officers over a period of years, just as we would for a person.

We might want to examine each deed to see who signed it on behalf of the company and the title that person held. Then we might want to run down that person's own personal transactions. We could similarly trace the names and backgrounds of all parties involved in property dealings with the company.

We could check records to see if a company is delinquent on its real estate and personal property taxes. Other records would show whether the company contracted with a governmental unit to supply goods or services. They would show whether the company sought a zoning change or applied for a permit to construct a new building or major addition.

We could discover from public records who handled a firm's rezoning request or public contracts and whether officers of the company contributed to political campaigns of public officials.

Next, people have children; corporations may set up subsidiaries or acquire them.

As individuals, we sometimes become involved in disputes that wind up in the courts. The same thing can happen to a company. We could examine records of state and federal courts to see if a given firm has been involved in litigation. There may be money judgments lodged against the firm. Or there might be court depositions that would disclose revealing information that otherwise might never have become open to public inspection.

Just as a person might do, a corporation may over-extend itself financially and face an array of creditors filing liens and claims. or it might be forced to file for bankruptcy in federal district court.

People get divorced; partnerships break up and companies sometimes sell off subsidairies or split up into several entities.

People die, and their passing is recorded in obituaries and death certificates. Similarly, corporations go out of business or file articles of dissolution with the state. Just as there may be a probate battle over a person's estate, a corporate demise may spawn litigation. All of this would be on the public record.

People work, get promoted, demoted and sometimes get fired. Corporations hire, promote, demote and fire people. A former employee, particularly a disgruntled one or an executive pushed out in a corporate power struggle, may prove a valuable source of information about a firm. Companies tend to publicize their managerial appointments, often sending out news releases for publication in local newspapers. Sometimes you can read between the lines and get an indication who the losers were in the corporate in-fighting.

When investigating a business firm, it often is helpful to concentrate on those things that set it apart from other businesses.

Consider its specific activities and the records that might be generated by what it does. A bank obviously has a far different set of functions than a real estate firm or insurance company.

Each of the three has activities that differ in some key respects from other businesses. Focus on those things that are distinct. List all the types of activities you might imagine a specific business would engage in. Then list what records — either private or public — these activities would produce.

Ask yourself which of these records you can reasonably expect to see. Some obviously will be unavailable to you. In such cases, who then might have access to them? What can you do to persuade a person who might have access to examine the documents and share some of the information with you?

You can succeed at this at times if you are imaginative and determined enough.

Most of us at one time or another have played verbal parlor games. In my investigative reporting classes, I have used a word-association game to encourage students to be as imaginative as possible.

One version began with a student being asked to designate a kind of business or occupation. The next student would then have to chip in a word, phrase or activity associated with the subject. As we worked our way around the class, each student added a new element related to the business or line of work initially selected.

Each student was to respond immediately. Once the tempo picked up and the class had been circled several times, there was virtually no room for reflection.

Then we would begin anew on the same subject, only this time around each student's response had to be directly related to the element or idea expressed by the preceding student. The purpose was to get each member of the class to itemize all of the impressions or activities he or she had of the given business or profession.

Throughout all these session, I consistently urged that students say the first thing that came to mind, regardless of how ridiculous or unrelated it might seem. It was an attempt to make them examine or reflect upon elements that might include the unconventional. Sometimes the most seemingly out-of-place idea might provide unexpected insight.

Once we had gone through these variations, we again returned to the designated occupation or business. Only this time, as one student offered a word or phrase, the next student had to come up with a type of record or document directly linked to the previous participant's choice.

For example, if the topic was an insurance firm and one student mentioned "car accident," the next student might cite a police accident report. Other potential responses might include an accident claim, autopsy report, personal injury damage suit, news media accounts of the accident or a record of penalty points being assessed against a driver's license. The next student would then introduce a new element or activity, with the following student coming up with a related record.

There was a final variation of the game. In this one, when a student cited a particular type of record, every member of the class would then either have to break down that record into its componemts, if any, or cite records akin to it.

For example, in the case of a personal injury suit, the other components might include statements of witnesses, a police accident report, court depositions, medical records, hospital and doctor billings, prior traffic records of the two drivers, and vehicular maintenance and inspection records.

As we went through these exercises, a listing would be kept of all the activities and records we had compiled, even those that might at first glance appear ludicrous. We would later review the listing and attempt to evaluate the merits of each response.

The results often were surprisingly comprehensive and promising. The virtue of this idea is that it prompts participants to think of the kinds of records that a given activity logically implies or requires.

One question invariably worth exploring is whether the corporation or business you are interested in is subject to regulation or supervision by local, state and/or federal agencies. If it is, such agencies' files might provide valuable information about the firm, its operations and how well it has complied with regulatory provisions.

"One question worth exploring is whether the business is subject to regulation or supervision by agencies."

A surprisingly large number of businesses fall into this category. Public utilities, for example, often are required to file annual or periodic reports with state and federal regulators. These include such agencies as state public service commissions, the Federal Power Commission, the Nuclear Regulatory Commission and the Federal Communications Commission.

The agency files also may include records and transcripts of hearings, the salaries of utility officers, data relating to proposed rate increases and documents and testimony submitted by the companies in support of their rate requests.

At the state level, the list of businesses subject to regulation may include banks, real estate and insurance firms, trucking and bus companies, privately-owned water and sewer companies, movers, nursing homes and fuel suppliers.

Many states that license real estate and insurance agents and brokers are likely to include in their files some background data on license applicants and firms they are authorized to represent. The agency often maintain files on complaints lodged by clients and consumer groups for possible investigation by the agency and disciplinary action.

Often a regulatory function of a municipality or state may include inspection services. Such reports by local and state building, fire, safety and health inspectors generally are public records and a potential gold mine of information. Their reports may disclose fire and sanitation hazards in restaurants and other public places, dangerous bridge and dam conditions, faulty construction practices, unsafe drinking water, abuse and mistreatment of hospital or nursing home patients, hazardous working conditions, and weight and volume cheating by supermarkets, gas stations and other businesses.

You may be able to talk to the inspectors themselves and enlist their aid or get additional details that they did not include in their reports.

Roy Malone and Terry Ganey, two St. Louis-Dispatch reporters, made extensive use of state inspection files when they wrote a lengthy series of articles disclosing appalling conditions and patient abuses in a number of nursing homes throughout Missouri.

Their articles also disclosed laxity by the state in allowing nursing homes to remain open despite having failed repeated inspections for sanitation, nursing care and fire safety. Malone and Ganey also found that some nursing homes were soaking the state on reimbursement payments by padding and falsifying their patient care expense reports.

Some nursing home operators, through an elaborate scheme of piling up loan, lease and mortgage costs, greatly padded their overhead expenses and thus got more money from the state. Some operators were offering $50 or more per person for each patient someone directed to their homes.

By reviewing state files kept in St. Louis, Malone was able to determine which nursing homes were substandard. Visits to these homes confirmed the safety hazards and poor nursing conditions, such as the elderly woman who was tied to her chair for such long periods that she lost the use of her legs. In many cases, employes of the homes and frustrated state inspectors were the best sources of information.

"Some nursing homes were soaking the state on reimbursement payments by padding their expense reports."

Malone learned about a wealthy old spinster from a small Missouri town who disappeared after being judged incompetent in a fast court action that denied her the right to effective counsel. Friends feared it was an attempt by relatives to take control of her money through guardianship. The friends did not even know in which state the nursing home was located.

Working with Illinois inspectors he befriended, Malone was able to locate the woman, who despite being afraid for her safety, proved to be lucid and well able to manage her affairs. He tape recorded her pleas for help and the tape was later played to her friends. An appeals court ruled that she was competent and she finally was able to return home.

Ganey, working in Jefferson City, the state capital, documented much of the financial and political manipulations of nursing home operators. The articles by the two reporters put pressure on the state legislature to revamp and strengthen Missouri's nursing home laws.

Uncle Sam, of course, takes a back seat to no one in the regulatory arena. His efforts span a vast array of regulatory activities including investment securities, the environment, consumer protection, rail and air travel, safety in the workplace, and private pension plans. The list would cover virtually every subject you can name.

The Federal Register, the official record of new and revised regulations, reflects the government's relentless expansion in this area. It grew to 61,000 pages in 1978, compared to 20,026 pages in 1970,

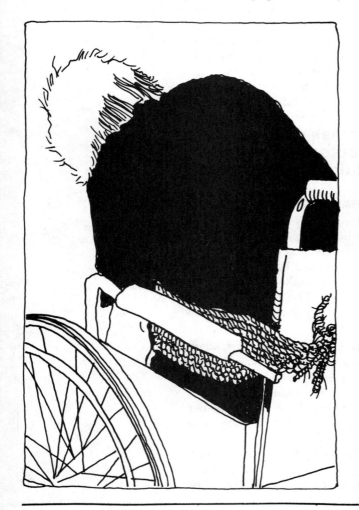

according to Congressional Quarterly. This growth prompted CQ to publish a Federal Regulatory Directory.

Its directory is well worth examining. The 1980-81 edition which runs 882 pages, bore a $25 pricetag. If you can't find a copy at your local library or bookstore, you could order one by writing Congressional Quarterly, Inc., 1414 22nd Street, NW, Washington, D.C., 20037.

The book contains extensive profiles of 15 of the largest, most important regulatory agencies, including their powers and authority and biographies of their commissioners or board members.

Another section of Congressional Quarterly's Federal Regulatory Directory covers 63 other important regulatory agencies, both the independent ones and those within executive departments. The section includes profiles of the agencies and their responsibilities, plus lists of telephone contacts, information sources and regional offices. There is also a comprehensive cross-reference index by subject and agency.

In his excellent book, "Investigative Reporting and Editing," the late Paul N. Williams cited the Office of Management and Budget in Washington as a good place to start to determine which agencies may be involved with a specific business you are investigating.

The federal office maintains an index of every type of report form required by federal agencies from more than 10 sources. Most of the agencies, Williams notes, gather their reports under the general theory of protecting the public health and safety.

A key regulatory agency in the business arena is the Securities and Exchange Commission, established in 1934. The agency is entrusted with trying to protect the integrity of much of the nation's business financing system.

It regulates securities trading on the 13 national securities exchanges and in the over-the-counter markets, as well as investigating securities frauds, stock and debenture manipulations, illegal corporate payoffs or political contributions.

As part of its job, the SEC requires public disclosure of pertinent data relating to most public offerings of securities. It also enforces disclosure requirements in the soliciting of proxies for security holder meetings of companies it regulates.

If you want information about a specific company that you believe might come under SEC jurisdiction, you might want to call the agency's nearest regional office to find out which office covers your state and ask which records may be on file.

There are regional offices in New York City, Boston, Atlanta, Chicago, Fort Worth, Denver and Los Angeles.

Under SEC rules, any company with more than 500 stockholders and more than $1 million in assets is required to make a public annual report to its stockholders.

SEC files include financial and other data submitted in registration statements, reports, applications and similar documents.

Some of the more important SEC reports, available in Washington or regional offices, include Form 3, the so-called "insider report." It requires that any officer, director or person holding more than 10 percent of a company's registered securities must file a report with the agnecy listing his or her full "beneficial ownership" of stock. Reports also must be filed for any month in which there was any change in their holdings.

Williams, in his book, "Investigative Reporting and Editing," suggests that Form S-1 is well worth examining. This is the registration form for companies first coming under SEC jurisdiction.

This document, Williams notes, "gives extensive detail about the formation of the company, the personal and business history of its officers, the capital structure, lines of credit and similar facts."

Among publications put out by the SEC is its News Digest. This is a daily report of important SEC developments. It includes agency announcements, decisions, orders, current reports and rules. The SEC also publishes a monthly summary of security transactions and holdings reported by company "insiders."

In the case of proposed stock and bond issues, you could check prospectuses filed with the SEC or your state securities division, depending on which agency has jurisdiction. The prospectuses often contain considerable financial details about the company involved.

Proxy statements that companies provide to stockholders prior to annual meetings are another good source of information. In the case of all corporations, they list the number of shares held by all directors, as well as any loans or financial transactions between a corporation and its directors. This often discloses holdings of top officers of a firm, since they frequently also serve as directors.

Hearings and records of Congressional and state legislative committees involving an industry or corporation can be a valuable source of information. Often you can obtain or examine hearing transcripts, as well as reports and studies by committee staff employees.

A directory of Congressional members, their staffs, committees and subcommittees has been published by Congressional Staff Directory, Limited, headed by Charles B. Bownson, who served eight years in Congress. The directory includes biographies of 2,800 staff members and data about Executive departments and federal agencies.

Congressional Quarterly has put out a "Washington Information Directory," which it says lists more than 5,000 sources in Congress, the Executive branch and private associations.

"Proxy statements that companies provide to stockholders are another good source of information."

If you can afford the tab, you might want to have an investment service company check out a firm you are interested in. Such companies frequently have excellent intelligence-gathering resources in the business arena, as well as being familiar with prospectuses and required financial public reports.

Two giants in the business information field are Moody's Investors Service, Inc., and Standard & Poor's Corp., both of New York. Moody's, for example, publishes a series of comprehensive annual manuals and twice-weekly news reports covering more than 18,000 corporations and institutions.

Moody's Transportation Manual provides

107

"But always remember that one's enemies may be so biased as to be unreliable."

specialized, highly-detailed information on more than 1,000 domestic transportation firms. Other manuals published by the firm include: Bank and Finance, covering more than 10,200 national, state and private banks, as well as data on insurance firms, investment companies and mutual funds: Industrial Manual, covering over 3,000 corporations listed on the American Stock Exchange and the New York Stock Exchange; OTC Industrial Manual, which includes data on more than 3,200 firms not listed on major exchanges, and a Public Utility Manual, which offers data on all publicly-held utility companies and many privately-held utilities.

In addition, Moody's publishes data on all issuers of commercial paper, including ratings and information for investors concerning the financial condition and operating trend of each issuer.

Local stockbrokers or financial analysts may be good to approach about a business firm you want to know more about. They have access to a lot of specialized information and often hear through the rumor mills things that never find their way into reports.

In checking out a business, it often is a good idea to talk to its competitors, customers and suppliers.

If you find a competitor incensed over how the business operates, try to draw out any details. But always remember that one's enemies may be so biased as to be unreliable. For this reason, you also should try to seek out the views of independent consultants or firms that compete in the same field but have no apparant ax to grind.

A company's suppliers can be a good source of information about whether a business pays its bills and honors its contractual obligations. Angry customers and suppliers may file complaints with the local chamber of commerce or Better Business Bureau. Or they may initiate court action.

Check local circuit courts, as well as federal courts

in your area, for possible lawsuits agaist the company you are investigating. In many jurisdictions, the courts maintain index cards or computer listings arranged alphabetically of all parties to lawsuits, both plaintiffs and respondents.

If there is a civil suit, examine all the documents filed. The files may disclose sources who could be helpful to you. If there are criminal charges filed against the company or its officers, you might attempt to broach law enforcement agencies involved and try to get more details about their investigation. If you have information you can "swap" with them, this might give you a little more leverage.

You also may want to talk to officers or members of unions involved in collective bargaining agreements with the business, particularly if the company has had a history of labor-management strife. Conversely, if you were investigating a union, you might want to seek out company sources who could give you a rundown on the union.

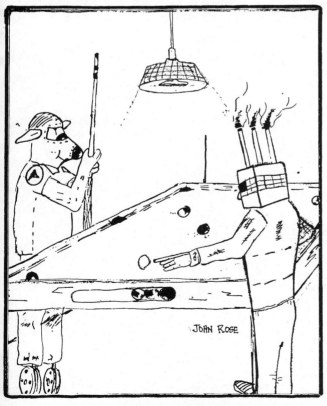

Details of Our Personal Lives Very Rarely Remain Private

WITHOUT our being aware of it, many details of our private lives are subject to scrutiny by people we never see. Their purposes often are legitimate, but at other times clearly unlawful.

We leave behind a trail of records that cannot always be protected against improper inspection and disclosure. Increasingly in recent decades, our society has gained ever more access to some of our daily doings, regardless of how private or personal they are.

Uncle Sam, for example, has been gathering data about American citizens, both collectively and as individuals, for a long time and funneling it into a complex of computers. Federal Government files bulge with data about our incomes, expenditures, health care and medical records, credit ratings, employment history and police records.

Some agencies have bent the law to their purpose. The Central Intelligence Agency, for example, reportedly amassed surveillance files on 10,000 American citizns in the United States in violation of the agency's charter.

Uncle Sam is not the only information-gatherer in our midst.

Each time we enter a department store or restaurant and make a credit card purchase, the record of our transaction is lodged somewhere. Our insurance records and medical expenditures and history may be open to inspection by unauthorized parties, despite elaborate safeguards designed to prevent this.

One example cited in Mademoiselle magazine was that of a surgeon who was hospitalized with a heart attack. After he returned home he found that his auto insurance had been cancelled. His agent said the insurer learned of the surgeon's heart trouble from a computerized hospital report.

In another instance, also reported in Mademoiselle, a man's employer "persuaded" him to drop a costly insurance claim for a work-related accident by mentioning the married employe's recent treatment for a venereal disease.

Police in some cities have spied on citizens.

In Seattle, for example, police allegedly compiled files on about 750 individuals and organizations prior to a 1979 city ordinance setting specific guidelines for police intelligence-gathering activities, according to a Parade magazine article.

None of those on the list had broken any laws or were suspected of criminal activity, the article said. Their ranks included not only anti-war demonstrators and political activists, but also businessmen, Indians, black construction workers and elected officials.

There are a number of steps you can take to protect both your privacy and reputation.

Under federal legislation, you have a right to examine credit bureau records relating to you. You also have a right to correct errors you might find in your file, or to at least explain in writing those entries you take exception to.

The law also includes criminal sanction to prohibit the release of credit data to unauthorized parties that might want to peruse your personal files.

Despite the safeguards, however, the system can and is being breeched. Some individuals, firms and private detective agencies have used friendly contacts and payoffs to credit office employes to get the information they seek.

At other times, they achieve the same result by having a company with a seemingly legitimate interest in your credit data obtain the information for them.

Even a layman sometimes can get to your credit and banking records by using this device or some similar subterfuge.

Do you want to know what kind of dossier the Federal Government may be keeping on you? The 1974 Privacy Act can be the vehicle you need.

In dealing with federal agencies, you have a right under the Privacy Act to inspect information about you that may be contained in their files. It also gives you the right to challenge the information there, as well as seeking to correct or amend it.

Passed by Congress to protect citizens from

invasion of privacy, the Act requires federal agencies to disclose to individuals the existence of data banks and files containing information on them. The Privacy Act is relatively easy to use.

You can send a letter to virtually any federal agency asking that it search its central files or any regional office files for any records that might involve you.

It is easy for most governmental units, law enforcement agencies, large detective agencies and major corporations to collect vast amounts of information relating to us as individuals. But they are not the only ones who can do it.

Even a schoolboy can at times have remarkable success in probing our private lives, as evidenced by the following article published in 1976 by the Chicago Sun-Times:

By Bob Olmstead
©1976, Chicago Sun-Times

Invading your privacy is easy. A snooper doesn't need private detectives, the FBI, the CIA or anybody else to get enough information to embarrass, discomfort or possibly endanger you.

It's so simple a child can do it — or to be more exact, a reasonably bright teenager. Ask David Hamlin, executive secretary of the American Civil Liberties Union, Illinois Division.

Hamlin found this out firsthand recently when he invited David Breskin, a 17 year-old New Trier West High School student, to invade his privacy by finding out everything he could about him. Breskin, a one-day-a-week intern in the ACLU's Chicago office, was working on the ACLU's current Privacy Project. Hamlin recalls, "I have always gone around telling people their privacy is not secure, so I thought it would be interesting to let him invade mine."

The ground rules were that the investigation was to be strictly one-citizen-spying-on-another, without spending money for outside help. But aside from that, said the ACLU director, "I told him he could work any way he wanted, as long as he didn't break the law."

Not everybody thinks privacy is important. Some people tell the ACLU, "My life is an open book. The only people who have anything to worry about are those who have something to hide."

Hamlin answers this in his soft-spoken but rapid-fire delivery: "I can tell you why privacy is important in three words: 'Information is power.' And the obvious corollary is: The more information you have about someone, the more power you have over them.

"The horror stories around here are endless. There's a local example, where police found out that someone attended a peace conference, passed this information on to a newspaper that published it, and the man was fired from his job.

"And it isn't only government. We have seen in this office a complaint from a single woman living with a male not her husband. She was denied auto insurance after an investigator found this out from a neighbor. The insurance company said that anyone who had no respect for a marriage contract would have no respect for an insurance

113

contract.

"And, of course, the worst thing about gossip is that it's not always true. But there is never any presumption of innocence in these things. Nobody asks the individual concerned.

"And, I'm afraid, there's no question but that our society is going in precisely the wrong direction. Because business and government assemble more than mere computerized information on people, we have more and more people who seem to feel we need more such information."

Hamlin sees privacy as an "elusive right" because it's not specifically stated in the Constitution. But he believes the Fourth Amendment protecting a citizen from unreasonable search and seizure is a start. "And increasingly I believe that anyone ought to have a warrant to violate my personal privacy."

Feeling the way he does, Hamlin was understandably shocked a couple of weeks after he gave Breskin his assignment when Breskin sat down in front of him, pulled out a page and a half of handwritten notes and laid out Hamlin's life for him. Said the ACLU pro: "It was scary."

These were Breskin's notes:

"Given: David Meriweather Hamlin, 217-44-7863. Born: June 5, 1945, in Washington, D.C. Past residences: Bethesda, Md.; Newark, N.J.; Philadelphia; Sanford, Me.; Concord, N.H.; Chicago; University of Maryland, 1963-1965, VISTA 1965-1966, Nasson College 1966-69.

"Personal: Hamlin makes about $18,000-$20,000 a year and has been working for ACLU in Chicago for a year and two weeks. He rents an apartment at 2970 N. Lake Shore Drive for $360 a month.

"According to informed sources, he is a very good tenant who has never caused any trouble. He is always on time with his payments and has been described as 'a very nice fellow.' No neighbors have complained about his behavior.

"He has a wife and a little boy, whom he takes 'everywhere' on weekends. Mrs. Hamlin seems to be a working mother, as she is never in during the day." (Note: Breskin's only assumption in the report was wrong. The Hamlins are separated.)

"The building he lives in is 20 years old, upper-class, and has 107 apartments.

"Occupation: Hamlin began training with VISTA 6-29-65 and ended training 8-9-65. He worked in the Philadelphia Bail Bond Project, which is now defunct. As a volunteer, he worked as a liaison with a detention center in preparation for release without bail of indigent prisoners and also did follow-up work after defendants release. Was under the directorship of Edmund DePaul, and terminated work 2-10-67. In Concord, he worked as executive director of New Hampshire ACLU.

"Finances: He opened an account with Amalgamated Bank in 10-74. Balances of under $1,000 have been maintained."

The student's notes also included the information, deleted here, that told how some of Hamlin's views disagreed with points of national ACLU policy, gave the times he leaves and enters his apartment each day, and provided his unlisted telephone number.

The investigation had taken about 25 hours of work.

Hamlin was astounded, irritated and soon to be mortified. When he asked how Breskin had gotten such stuff, Breskin was obliged to tell him that Hamlin himself had unknowingly given out about one-fifth of it because he had fallen for a ruse. The student had mailed Hamlin a fake questionnaire and Hamlin, guardian of privacy, had dutifully filled it out and sent it back.

Admittedly, Breskin got some of the information from snooping in the ACLU office — but he said he didn't have to snoop very hard and he believes any ordinary citizen could have gotten the same information out of the ACLU, a comparatively open organization. It was there that he got Hamlin's salary, phone number and address.

After snooping in the ACLU office, Breskin — who has a pleasantly self confident voice that makes him sound years older than he is — next picked up the phone and called Hamlin's apartment building for some personal information.

He said his first call, outside business hours, was answered by a janitor, who gave a general description of the building without asking for any kind of identification or explanation. The next time he called, he said, he talked with a woman who identified herself as the building's manager.

"I told her that I was a prospective employer of Mr. Hamlin and that I just wanted to get a little background information on him — because we have to be careful. I asked her how much his apartment rented for and she said about $360 a month."

When the woman ran out of answers to his questions, Breskin said, "She said the doorman might know something, so she put the doorman on the phone." Just as the doormen do in the implausible detective stories, the doorman told Breskin all about Hamlin's personal habits without apparently worrying whether he might be talking to a prospective burglar or perhaps a kidnaper.

If you believe your apartment manager or neighbors wouldn't talk like bluejays, don't be too sure. Several detective agencies later told Breskin that such chattiness is common.

"Mostly," said Breskin, "what the private investigators told me was that the most you can find out about someone is through people who know the person — neighbors, friends, office workers — that's where most of your information can come from. It just depends on how much time you have and, in some cases, how much money.

"And a couple of them described the human psychology of it — that people just love to be inside something. When they feel something's going on, they just volunteer information. You know: 'So-and-so was having a party on such-and-such a night and . . .' That type of thing, which can be very, very damaging."

Next, Breskin telephoned VISTA headquarters in Washington, D.C. "I told them I was doing a research project on VISTA volunteers. I didn't ask about anybody else besides Hamlin." Over the telephone, VISTA gave Breskin the gist of Hamlin's career as a volunteer, although nothing so chatty as Hamlin's landlords.

In his attempt to get at Hamlin's finances, Breskin first tried the direct approach. He asked an ACLU secretary where her boss banked, and then called up the Amalgamated Trust and Savings Bank, and asked if personnel would tell him how much Hamlin kept in his checking account. "They said I was nuts. There was no way."

But there was a way. Breskin simply asked a family friend in a brokerage house to write a letter to Amalgamated, asking for the same information on the fictitious grounds that Hamlin had just opened an account at the brokerage firm.

Amalgamated sent back a form letter stating that Hamln's checking account, opened in October, 1974, had generally averaged a balance of "moderate 3," or, as the code was translated, less than $1,000.

At this point, Breskin was winding up his research and wanted to fill in some holes. And what better source to fill in the holes than Hamlin himself. So, he said, "I sent the now infamous letter."

The letter came from New Trier High School's FM radio station, WNTH, where Breskin also works and had arranged the hoax with Jeff Goldberg, the director who signed the letter.

"In the letter, I (Breskin) said that we at the station were dismayed at Walter Jacobson's (critical television) commentary that said no one cares about the ACLU. I said that we certainly do care about the ACLU, and that we wanted to do a documentary on the ACLU, and it would be nice to get some background on him. Of course, the ACLU is always looking for publicity, so that's a trap."

Hamlin jumped into the trap with both feet. "We are delighted with your supportive response," he wrote back. "I have taken the liberty of circulating your letter to our staff, all of whom will be pleased to know that you do, indeed, care."

Breskin was shrewd enough to fill the questionnaire mostly with big, soft questions that Hamlin couldn't resist hitting out of the ball park, such as, "What have been the most important ACLU decisions in the past decade?" He also slipped in three for his own purpose: "How long have you worked for the ACLU? What is your background in law or civil liberties legislation? How did you first become interested in the ACLU?"

Hamlin said that falling for the questionnaire was doubly embarrassing because Breskin had in effect warned him beforehand by telling him that private investigators told him the best source of information on a person is often the person himself.

In restrospect, what do people who talked so freely about Hamlin say now? "Some were much less talkative when I called them."

At Hamlin's apartment building, a woman who said she was the new acting manager said she gives out no information about her tennants. "No building would," she said. Told that the former building manager apparently did, she said she didn't know about that and couldn't comment.

At VISTA's Washington records office, a spokesman said VISTA is allowed to give out a former volunteer's name, dates of service, and the name and general description of the project. He said he had no idea of how Breskin got the name of Hamlin's director and the description of his duties. "I'd like to know who he talked with myself," he said.

A spokesman for Amalgamated Bank, who declined to be named, said only, "Our official policy is to protect our customers and I don't want to say anything more."

And what about not the least of those who blabbed about David Hamlin — David Hamlin himself?

"I've learned my lesson," he said. "I intend to be a little more careful — and not just when the obvious circumstances comes up, when somebody asks for my social security number.

"Breskin pointed out that the best source of information is the person himself, and I, for one, intend to believe him.

"What I wanted David to do was to prove that I was not as private a person as I thought I was — and he sure as hell did that."

An Act of Congress Lets YOU Discover What THEY Know

THE Freedom of Information Act (FOI) has been a real boon to investigators and researchers since its adoption by Congress in 1966.

Often it provides the only avenue open to us for ferreting out secret misdeeds and bizarre actions by federal agencies. It also gives us a chance to find out what files, if any, the federal bureaucracy may be keeping on us or on groups we belong to.

Without the act, we might never have learned that:

♦The Central Intelligence Agency performed "behavior control" experiments on unsuspecting victims during the Cold War, using Americans in prisons as guinea pigs and using the nation's universities as research centers. The techniques included use of "mind-bending" and memory-erasing drugs.

Among the more than 1,000 pages of documents the CIA was forced to release under the FOI Act was a letter written in 1949 by a CIA operative. It outlined ways agents could commit murder without getting caught, including deep-freezing victims, X-raying them to death and strangling them with a bath towel.

♦The Federal Bureau of Investigation put out a bogus newsletter in St. Louis in 1969 containing smears about the sex lives of area civil rights figures as part of a scheme to harass and discredit them. The FBI later claimed that at least two civil rights figures were discredited by the bogus publication, while another one was "destroyed."

The documents detailed FBI efforts to harass and disrupt black militants and leftist organizations. In one instance, agents tried to break up a black leader's marriage by writing a poison-pen letter to his wife.

♦After being forced to resign from office, former President Richard M. Nixon used his federal annual allowance of $150,000 to buy such items as electric

117

golf carts, telephone taping equipment and a subscription to The Washington Post. The Post had won a Pulitizer Prize for its reports on the Watergate scandal.

♦Several days after Ernest Hemingway committed suicide in the summer of 1961, the FBI took note of his death by inserting a clipping of a hostile obituary into a thick file folder it had kept on Hemingway. The agency's file dated back to 1942 and showed that, in effect, the U.S. Government had once declared Hemingway to be subversive.

Hemingway's almost paranoid fears of FBI harassment, the file showed, had been exaggerated, but were not entirely unfounded, one researcher concluded.

♦Both the FBI and CIA kept files on the Rev. Robert F. Drinan, a Catholic priest elected to Congress in 1970. The 18-page CIA file included a review of a baccalaureate address Drinan gave in 1973 at Sweet Briar College in Virginia. The file referred to his support of student protests "over the Kent State deaths and the invasion of Cambodia." It also noted that Drinan urged the abolition of all secret government files, including CIA files.

The FBI dossier on Drinan covered 81 pages and dated to 1958 when he was dean of the Boston College law school and active in the civil rights movement. The files contained references to lawyers' groups he had worked with to protect civil liberties of southern blacks. Also included were reports on anti-war speeches he had given.

Using the FOI Act, Drinan got to see copies of both agencies's files on him in 1975. His cost: $8.10, according to a wire news service.

In 1976, a New Jersey newspaper disclosed that known cancer-causing agents had been found in the air near five north Jersey industrial areas. It cited the chemical agents and plant locations involved. The paper used an FOI request to obtain an Environmental Protection Agency report that contained the findings.

A former researcher at Harvard University used the act to obtain a series of federal audit reports that disclosed a widespread pattern of sloppy bookkeeping and alleged misuse of federal research funds, involving hundreds of millions of dollars, by colleges and universities across the country.

The researcher made the documents available to The New York Times, which then publicized the audit findings and conclusions.

The at-times controversial Church of Scientology has made effective use of the FOI act to expose CIA misdeeds and experiments in mind control. In one of its publications, the Church of Scientology said that documents it obtained through the Freedom of Information Act showed that dangerous biological warfare tests were conducted in 1969, less than 50 miles from the White House.

The tests, it asserted, were part of larger pattern of chemical-biological warfare experiments carried out by the military in several eastern coastal cities between 1951 and 1969. The article said the documents showed Army scientists sprayed potentially hazardous zinc cadmium sulfide over the Cambridge, Md., area in massive open air tests in 1969.

Since its enactment, the Freedom of Information Act has helped citizens open to public view tens of thousands of previously secret files, including massive files relating to the espionage convictions of Ethel and Julius Rosenberg.

Imagine the shock and outrage felt by William Beecher, a top-flight reporter and news correspondent, when he filed an FOI request and later began receiving more than a foot-high stack of copies of documents that disclosed a massive invasion of his privacy and civil rights by federal agencies.

In one day's mail, he received 280 pages of FBI reports summarizing wiretaps placed on his telephone by the agency for a nine-month period ending in early 1971. He got to read the heavily-censored reports five years after his home phone had been tapped.

Beecher also discovered that extensive files had been kept on him by other agencies, including the CIA, the Department of Defense, the Department of State, the National Security Council and the Secret Service.

Beecher, a former reporter for the Wall Street Journal and The New York Times, wrote about his feelings of outrage in a lengthy article in the Boston Globe in 1976. He had become the Globe's diplomatic correspondent.

"And what was the heinous activity being investigated by all these over-worked agencies of government?" Beecher asked. "I have been a Washington correspondent 15 years and some of the articles I wrote over that span incurred the displeasure of Presidents, Cabinet officers and others who were determined to discover my sources, presumably so they could shut them up."

Beecher said he first experienced an eerie feeling when he learned about the phone taps.

But this was quickly replaced, he said, by "deep boiling anger over the realization that federal officials could eavesdrop on my most personal, intimate conversations with my wife, with relatives, with friends and dutifully type out reports of what they regarded as significant, or interesting, or merely titillating, for higher-ups to paw over."

Why were the wiretaps initiated? Beecher never was given any official explanation. One knowledgeable reporter, however, attributed it to a story Beecher wrote in May 1970 in which he disclosed there had been very heavy American air strikes into North Vietnam during the so-called bombing halt.

Earlier, he had written a story detailing secret B-52 bombing in Cambodia. And later Beecher angered Nixon Administration officials with a 1971 story in the New York Times spelling out details of the SALT talks status and some United States proposals.

The scope of federal efforts, including CIA probes, to uncover his possible sources was both puzzling and disturbing to Beecher. "It's enough to make a sane

man paranoiac," he wrote. "Or a sane society."

Journalists, researchers and reputable private citizens are not the only persons who have made use of the Freedom of Information Act.

Some criminals have sought to benefit from it. A convicted loan shark, for example, testified at a Senate subcommittee hearing a few years ago that he used the FOI Act in an attempt to find out what the government knew about him and where it was getting the information.

The convict, Gary Bowdach, told the Senate subcommittee that although he was never able to identify the informants who were supplying information in his case, he learned of an informant who tattled on one of his friends. He told the senators he also had used the FOI Act to find out whether a federal agency had an investigation pending against him.

The Freedom of Information Act gives "any person" access to *all* records of *all* agencies, unless these records fall within one of nine exempt categories. In these latter instances, the agencies involved are permitted — but not required — to withhold the information.

You can make an informal telephone request for the data or documents you need. If that doesn't work, you can file a formal written request. Once you make such a request, the burden is on the federal agency or government to promptly provide you with the documents or show that they fall within an exempt category.

On receipt of a formal request, the federal agency has 10 working days to either provide the information you require or to respond. If the agency refuses release of all or part of the information sought, you may appeal to the agency head.

Denial of your appeal or failure to reply in 20 working days gives you the right to file suit in the federal court nearest you. If you win the lawsuit, the judge would direct the agency to release the information, as well as ordering it to pay your attorney fees and court costs.

The FOI Act covers all federal agencies and even government-controlled corporations such as the Postal Service and Amtrak. Not covered by the Act are the federal courts, Congress, the President and his immediate staff — although the Executive Office of the President is.

The "records" available include documents of all kinds: papers, reports, letters, films, photographs, sound recordings and computer tapes. You must describe the material you want. All U.S. citizens and foreign nationals can use the FOI Act, as well as any corporation, partnership or other entity.

If you decide to make a informal telephone request, call the agency's public information or press officer. If you are turned down, call the agency's FOI officer. As an added persuader, let it be known that you will file a formal request, as well as an appeal and lawsuit if necessary to get the data or documents.

Large cabinet agencies, such as Defense and Agriculture, have separate FOI officers in their regional offices and various subdivisions. If you know a subdivision or regional office has the records you seek, you may send your request directly to that FOI officer. If you don't know which federal agency has the records, you may have to send formal requests to several agencies.

The envelope that encloses your request should be marked, "FOI Act Request." The letter should be sent by registered mail, with return receipt requested. Be sure to retain a photostatic copy of the letter.

In the body of the letter, state that your request is being made under federal FOI Act, 5 U.S.C. 552. Then describe clearly what material you want. Include names, places and the period of time about which you are inquiring. Be as specific as possible about what you want. At the end of this section, we will include an actual request letter that illustrates how to be both concise and comprehensive.

In your letter state that you expect to be sent all non-exempt parts of the requested records, as well as justification for any deletions. You may attach documents to describe the subject of your inquiry. You might want to state your intention to appeal any decision to withhold.

You must agree to pay any reasonable fees involved in the search for materials you request. Ask to be notified, preferably by telephone, if the agency estimates the fees will exceed a certain dollar limit. You could then decide what it might cost to further pursue your inquiry. Perhaps you might want to narrow its scope or the number of documents sought.

If you are a journalist, researcher or author planning to use the information you get in a publication, ask the agency to waive or reduce search and copying fees. You should stress that the data you are requesting would "primarily benefit the general public." Waiver requests can also be made by indigents and non-profit groups.

At times, you may find it quicker and cheaper to visit the agency and ask to examine the documents you are interested in, rather than having them copied and forwarded to you.

The reference department of your public library might be a good place to find the names, addresses and telephone numbers of federal agencies covered

"You have a right to appeal to an Agency head if your FOI request is denied."

by the FOI Act. Or check the federal office listings in your local phone directory.

Congressional Quarterly publishes a Washington Information Directory. It provides a wealth of information about the federal government. Included is a list of telephone numbers of FOI contacts at major federal agencies and departments.

A very helpful guidebook to use of the FOI Act has been published by the FOI Service Center. The booklet is a joint project of the Reporters Committee for Freedom of the Press and the Society of Professional Journalists, Sigma Delta Chi. It includes sample letters, forms and a directory of some major agency FOI phone numbers and addresses. It also has a section on the Privacy Act.

At this writing, the booklet is being distributed at 50 cents a copy. You can request one by writing the FOI Service Center, c/o the Reporters Committee for Freedom of the Press, 1125-15th Street, N.W., Washington, D.C., 20005. The FOI Service Center is also available to provide additional assistance to journalists.

The booklet includes a schedule of fees charged by some federal agencies relative to FOI requests. A few agencies, such as the Civil Aeronautics Board, might not charge fees. Most do, however. Search fees usually run $4 to $6 an hour for clerical personnel and from $10 to $18 an hour for professional employees. Computer-time fees vary greatly, but often run $60-$70 an hour. The cost of photocopying generally is 10 cents a page.

You may be charged search fees even if few or no documents that you request are found. Under the FOI Act, agencies are required to publish in the Federal Register uniform schedules for search and reproduction fees.

As noted earlier, you have a right to appeal to the agency head if your FOI request is wholly or partially denied. If there is a partial denial, it often is a good idea to accept what documents you can get and appeal the rest.

Even if your request is granted, you can appeal if you feel the fees charged are excessive. Or you can appeal if 10 business days have passed and you have not received a reply from the agency. The agency has the right to notify you in advance if unusual circumstances make it necessary to have more time available for research.

You should be aware that the courts often give exemptions on the response deadlines to certain agencies such as the FBI, CIA and the Justice and State Departments because of the volume and backlog of requests.

Negotiation by telephone with the agency FOI officer is often helpful before making a formal appeal. You may be able to arrive at a compromise and get some of the denied documents released.

If you are unsuccessful, however, a formal appeal may be critical. It is the only way that you can put the agency under a legal burden to review your request and is also needed to establish your right to file a lawsuit if the appeal is denied. Your appeal need only be a brief letter reviewing your request and denial. Copies of any correspondence should be attached. The appeal should be addressed to the agency administrator. State your belief that the denial was unjustified and list your arguments in support of this view. You should also make it clear you intend to file suit if the denial is upheld.

You can file suit in the United States District Court nearest you if the appeal is denied or if the agency fails to respond to your appeal within 20 working days. If your case is routine, there is a short-form complaint you can use. But you may want to confer with and retain an attorney if your case is complicated or involves special problems.

It is a good idea to learn which officials are particularly responsible for withholding documents you have requested. This is because you may want to refer to FOI Act punitive provisions while talking with any agency personnel. The Act provides that responsible agency employees can be subject to disciplinary action for "arbitrary" or "capricious" withholding of information. Such disciplinary steps, however, have been rare.

As an alternative to filing a lawsuit, you may ask for an informal review of your case by the U.S. Justice Department's Office of Information and Law. This is the agency currently ressonsible for the general administration of the FOI Act. You must, however, contact the agency prior to filing suit.

"Under the FOI Act, there are nine reasons the government can refuse to disclose information."

Under the Freedom of Information Act, there are nine exemptions or reasons the government can refuse to disclose information. They are:

♦ National security, where release of records would cause "identifiable damage" to the nation.

♦ Internal personnel practices.

♦ Information specifically exempted by law — the "catch-all exemption."

♦ Trade secrets or other confidential financial or commercial information.

♦ Inter-agency or intra-agency memos.

♦ Personal privacy, including personnel or medical files.

♦ Law enforcement investigations — current and pending files only.

♦ Federally-regulated bank reports — little used exemption which limits disclosure of sensitive financial reports which might undermine confidence in individual banks.

♦ Geological and geophysical information — oil and gas wells.

Since enactment of the Freedom of Information Act in 1966 and a series of key amendments eight years later, thousands of individuals and organizations aggressively have sought information and documents under its provisions. The Church of Scientology has been among those effectively using the Act.

The following FOI request by Susan Worstell, director of public affairs of the Church of Scientology of Missouri, is being reprinted with permission. It is included here because it illustrates how well such a request can be written. It is comprehensive, yet

127

concise and specific. In her request, she clearly sets forth what she is seeking, while at the same time making a broad appeal for documents and other records.

The letter:

FREEDOM
The Independent Journal Published
by the Church of Scientology

Department of the Army
Office for the Freedom of
  Information, OCP-OSA
The Pentagon
Washington D.C. 20330
202-697-4122

13 December 1980

Dear Sir:

This is a request under the Freedom of Information ACT as amended (5 U.S.C. 552).

I am writing representing FREEDOM, The Independent Journal published by the Church of Scientology, to request copies of any and all directives, memoranda, letters or other records, including written memoranda of telephone conversations, which relate to the establishment of programs or plans concerning the testing and/or use of chemical and biological warfare agents and/or agents in the testing of mind control techniques in the states of Missouri, Kansas, Illinois, and Nebraska, Tennessee and Kentucky during the years of 1950 through 1980.

Previous documentation received under this act has dealt with 1) open air tests including aerosol clouds within cities 2) the breeding of insects carrying deadly diseases e.g. mosquites carrying yellow fever 3) the spraying of Agent Orange 4) use of volunteers, knowlingly or unknowingly, receiving experimental drugs e.g. BZ, LSD 5) the releasing of chemical agents by dropping capsules in certain populated areas. We are herewith requesting documentation on tests of this nature, proposed or carried out, including but not limited to these type of testing techniques, during the times and within the areas afore mentioned.

We would also like any further information on a particular series of tests done in Minneapolis, St. Louis, and Winnipeg which started in 1953. These tests, conducted by the Chemical Corp of the US Army, were entitled "Behavior of Aerosol Clouds within Cities." A copy of the cover sheet for copy 30 of 30, Series A Joint Quarterly Report No 4 is attached for your reference. A complete copy of this report is in our possession. We wish to have copies of any prior or subsequent reports.

Specific areas of interest in this series of tests are the participation of the Monsanto Company of St. Louis, Mo., Socony-Vacuum Refining Co., East St. Louis Ill., Granite City Steel Co., Illinois, and the Ralph H. Parsens Company.

We would also like transcripts relating the circumstances and details discussed in the meetings with city officials in St. Louis including the St. Louis Fire and Police Departments, the Mayor's Office, and members of the Park Board concerning said experiments carried out in St. Louis. (See attached copy of document, #2).

Accordng to the above mentioned document, "All microscopic analysis, computation of dosages, plotting of dosage distribution and wind flow maps were done in the Minneapolis office." (page 31 of documents, copy enclosed #3) This might assist in locating the requested documentation on these tests.

A reference to a subsequent report to be written on the analysis of the tests is on page 24 which says, "detailed decriptions of these sites will be included in a subsequent quarterly report covering summer operations in St. Louis." We would like a copy of this report also. (See enclosure #4)

Finally, we would like any information on the use of NJZ 2266-Zinc cadmium sulfide in chemical testing of any type as outlined above.

In the unlikely event that access is denied to any part of the requested records, please describe the deleted material in detail and specify the statutory bases for the denial as well as your reasons for believing that the alleged statutory justification applies in this instance. Please separately state your reasons for not invoking your discretionary powers to release the requested documents in the public interest. Such statements will be helpful to us in deciding whether to appeal an adverse determination, and in formulating our arguments in case we might possibly avoid unnecessary litigation.

We anticipate, however, that you will make the requested materials available to us within the statutory prescribed period of ten (10) working days.

We also request that you waive any applicable fees since disclosure meets the statutory standard for waiver of fees in that it would clearly be "In the public interest because furnishing the information can be considered as primarily benefiting the general public. "In this regard, we further point out that FREEDOM News Service is a nonprofit news organization which intends to give the requested information the widest possible circulation.

We await your prompt reply.

Susan Worstell
St. Louis Bureau
FREEDOM News Service

Afterword

Everyone has a right to take those steps that are lawfully open to him in protecting himself in dealings with others, whether they be friends, strangers or enemies. By law, everyone also has a right to examine scores of public records relating to individuals, corporations and institutions.

But there are limits — both legal and ethical — that should not be exceeded.

We do not have any guaranteed right to needlessly probe or divulge details of an individual's personal life. Mere curiosity does not give us the right to invade the privacy of a person or firm whose activities do not thrust them into the public arena.

We have no right to libel or slander someone.

In a long career as a newspaper reporter, I have steadfastly sought to refrain from delving into the private lives of individuals. I have done so on some occasions, but only when I felt it was necessary because the person's private life could not be separated from a clearly public issue. Invariably the persons involved were public officials or were doing business with governmental agencies.

It is true that there is little left of privacy in today's world, given the enormous information-gathering forces at work in our midst. That does not mean, however, that we are justified in invading someone else's privacy without the most compelling reason.

This book has been intended as an investigative primer for the lay person and any interested journalist.

Time and again, I have tried to emphasize that there is no single approach that will guarantee success in every investigative effort. But I am convinced that the principles outlined here can help provide such success, particularly if one is willing to devote the time and mental effort needed.

If you are stubborn and determined to get to the bottom of something, your chances of success are that much better. When Carl Bernstein and Bob Woodward began their Watergate investigation, each had good reporting credentials. But they were not as widely known or acclaimed as other journalistic stars who did not pursue the Watergate scandal with the same passion they did. The two reporters succeeded largely because of hard work and sheer determination and because their editors believed in the importance of what they were doing.

In any investigation, the facts are what counts. We must not distort or ignore facts that do not fit our pre-conceived notions or theories. We may sense that something is wrong or improper; all our instincts and research may suggest this is the case. But unless we can adequately document and prove it, we have no right to bend or force our findings to suit our ends or possible prejudices.

Patience is a key virtue. Sometimes if we keep at a project long enough, we will find the missing piece or documentation that we need. Often we have to put things on a "back burner" for a while and wait to see what develops.

Change is one of the few things assured in life. As this is written, for example, the federal Freedom of Information Act is under attack by some officials in the Reagan Administration and by some governmental agencies, such as the CIA and the FBI, that want to restrict public access to their files. Only time will tell what success they will have. They may push through some revisions, but there is no guarantee these changes will not be later set aside or amended.

So, too, in the area of public records and the manner in which they are kept. The scope of records available to us may alternately be cut back and expanded. The records themselves may become increasingly automated under technologies that are as yet still on the drawing boards. But the principles we have discussed in this book about how to identify and trace records are not likely to be soon invalidated. If anything, the flood of records will continue to increase.

Further Reading

INVESTIGATIVE REPORTING AND EDITING, by Paul N. Williams. Prentice-Hall, Inc., Englewood Cliffs, N.Y. 07632 (1978)

THE INVESTIGATIVE JOURNALIST: FOLK HEROES OF A NEW ERA, by James H. Dygert. Prentice-Hall, Inc., Englewood Cliffs, N.J. 07632 (1976)

THE IRE JOURNAL, published every other month by Investigative Reporters and Editors, Inc., 100 Neff Hall, School of Journalism, University of Missouri, Mo., 65211

THE REPORTER'S HANDBOOK, Investigative Reporters & Editors, Inc., (IRE) under the editorship of John Ullmann and Steve Honeyman, St. Martin's Press, New York, NY. 1983

THE NEW PRECISION JOURNALISM, by Philip Meyer, Indiana University Press, 273 pages (1991) An updated version of Meyer's 1973 classic, which also was updated in 1978.

THE JOURNALISM OF OUTRAGE: Investigative Reporting and Agenda Building in America, by David L. Protess and co-authors Fay Lomax Cook, Jack C. Doppelt, James S. Ettema, Margaret T. Gordon, Donna R. Leff and Peter Miller. Guilford Press, 72 Spring Street, New York, NY., 10012

McCLURE'S MAGAZINE AND THE MUCKRAKERS, by Harold S. Wilson, Princeton, New Jersey, Princeton University Press, 1970.

INVESTIGATIVE REPORTING by Clark R. Mollenhoff, Macmillan Publishing Co., Inc., New York (1981).

TRADE SECRETS OF WASHINGTON JOURNALISTS, by Steve Weinberg, Acropolis Books, Ltd., Washington, D.C. (1981)

INVESTIGATIVE REPORTING, by David Anderson and Peter Benjaminson, Indiana University Press, Bloomington, Ind. (1976).

About The Author

Louis J. Rose is an investigative reporter with more than 33 years in newspapering.

He is considered by his editors and fellow reporters as an expert in digging out stories of corporate, governmental and individual corruption by using records and cultivating sources.

A native of New Bedford, Mass., he is a graduate of Bates College, Lewiston, Me., and earned a master's degree in journalism from the Medill Graduate School of Journalism at Northwestern University, Evanston, Ill.

He has worked for the Terre Haute (Ind.) Star and the Providence Journal-Bulletin. Rose joined the Post-Dispatch news staff in 1964. During his years as a reporter, he has covered state and local government in considerable depth. His work documenting governmental fraud, political corruption, conflicts of interest and favoritism has exposed and helped to stop practices costing taxpayers millions of dollars. In a carefully documented series involving six months of work, he uncovered widespread jobshirking by St. Louis city employees who were "goofing off" elsewhere, instead of doing their jobs.

His work in documenting long-standing court leniency in handling of drunk-driving cases in Missouri earned him a special Gavel award from the American Bar Association.

Rose spent about one and one-half years with two colleagues on an award-winning series that disclosed how nuclear waste had been created and secretly disposed of in the St. Louis area, causing widespread contamination.

He was nominated for a Pulitzer Prize for 1991 with fellow reporter Tim Poor, for their year-long investigation that disclosed abuses by local and state police and federal agencies, in the seizure and forfeiture of tens of millions of dollars in cash, cars and other property from alleged drug suspects—many of them innocent people. Often those arrested had only small amounts of drugs, and often were never convicted or even charged.

Rose long has been active in Investigative Reporters & Editors, Inc. and is a past president of the St. Louis chapter of the Society of Professional Journalists. He and his wife, Carol, live in a St. Louis suburb. They are the parents of three children.

Acknowledgements

An investigative reporter needs the cooperation of others if he is to be successful. This is no less true in the effort to produce this book.

This book is due to my wife, Carol, who helped me conceive the idea for the book and gave so much support in the writing and marketing involved. I am also indebted to the patience and understanding of our three children—Leslie, John and Neil. Without them, this effort probably would not have progressed beyond the talking stage.

And to my colleagues at the St. Louis Post-Dispatch I owe a great debt of gratitude. Many friends and associates at this fine newspaper, now in its third generation of Pulitzer leadership, have given freely of their time and advice.

Special thanks are due four friends who gave so much help in the editing, design and layout of this book:

Co-Editors: Larry Fiquette and Robert J. Byrne

Art Editor: Ed Kohorst

Layout and design: Ellen Gardner

(Cover design and all illustrations by Kohorst, except as otherwise credited.)

ISBN: 0-9606846-2-X